THE LOST SWEDISH TRIBE

Reapproaching the history of Gammalsvenskby in Ukraine

Edited by Piotr Wawrzeniuk
& Julia Malitska

©The Authors

Södertörn University
SE-141 89 Huddinge

www.sh.se/publications

Cover Design: Jonathan Robson
Layout: Per Lindblom & Jonathan Robson

Printed by Elanders, Stockholm 2014

Research Report 2014:1
ISSN 1403-5111
ISBN 978-91-86069-85-8

Contents

Acknowledgements   5

Approaching the "Lost Swedish Tribe" in Ukraine
PIOTR WAWRZENIUK & JULIA MALITSKA   13

The Russian State and Swedes in New Russia
(between the eighteenth and nineteenth centuries)
SVITLANA BOBYLEVA   39

People in between
– Baltic islanders as colonists on the steppe
JULIA MALITSKA   61

The making of Gammalsvenskby 1881–1914
– identity, myth and imagination
PIOTR WAWRZENIUK   89

Little Red Sweden in Ukraine
– the 1930s Comintern project in Gammalsvenskby
ANDREJ KOTLJARCHUK   111

About the authors   151

List of tables

Table 1: Number of families in the Swedish colonist district (1800–1887). (**p. 50**)

List of figures

Figure 1: The population of Gammalsvenskby 1781–1929. (**p. 62**)

List of documents

Document 1: The Imperial Decree of Catherine II to the Estonian governor general board about the resettlement of the peasants of the manor of Körgessaare (Hohenholm) to New Russia province, 8 March, 1781. (**p. 30**)

Document 2: About the Swedish colonies in remote parts of Russia. (**p. 40**)

Document 3: A fragment of Emmanuel Richelieu's letter to Samuel Contenius, 9 April, 1806. (**p. 67**)

Document 4: Samuel Contenius's report to governor-general Emmanuel Richelieu about the lack of bread in Molochna, the Swedish and Odessa colonies and with regards to this paying food money to the colonists, 17 November, 1806. (**p. 67/8**)

Document 5: About bad harvests in 1899 in the Swedish colony. (**p. 76**)

Document 6: The report by the Scandinavian *Ländersekretariat* concerning the Old-Swedish immigrants in Sweden. (**p. 117**)

Document 7: Recommendation from the Politburo of the Swedish Communist Party (*Sveriges Kommunistiska Parti* or *SKP*) to comrade Hugo Lauenstein issued by SKP, certified by Edvin Blom, 7 October, 1932. (**p. 134**)

List of maps

Map 1: *Tataria Minor cum Adiacentibus Kiovensi et Belgorodensi Guberniis*, 1745. (**p. 10**)

Map 2: *Mappa Generalis Gubernii Novae Russiae in Circulos Divisi 1779 Suctore.* (**p. 11**)

Map 3: *Der Hapsalsche Kreis*, 1802. (**p. 12**)

Map 4: *Cherson Region*, circa 1789–1805. (**p. 36**)

Map 5: *Spets. Karta Zap. Chasti Rossiiskoi Imperii G.L. Schuberta*, 1826–1840. (**p. 37**)

Map 6: *Plan of Kazykermen [Kezikermen] district of Kazykermen province divided into lots for Swedish peasants from Estonia*, 1781. (**p. 59**)

Map 7: *Etnograficheskaia karta Rossiiskoi Imperii*, 1851. (**p. 60**)

Acknowledgements

Researchers and authors inevitably become indebted to many people during the course of a project spanning over several years. The most important agent behind the research presented in this anthology is The Foundation for Baltic and East European Studies (*Östersjöstiftelsen*), the main sponsor of our undertakings. The Swedish Institute (*Svenska institutet*) contributed with additional funding for the pre-development of the project, for stipends to individual researchers, and for a workshop. In addition, an important contribution that facilitated the documentation process was made by Helge Ax:son Johnson's Foundation. For all that, we are very grateful.

The research team is also indebted to the management and staff of the State Archives in Odessa and Kherson, and a large group of helpful archivists and librarians from Ukraine in the south to Sweden and Finland in the north. We would, in particular, like to thank Bertil Olofsson at Krigsarkivet, Stockholm.

The texts in the anthology were, in various versions, put forward at research seminars and workshops at Södertörn University, Sweden, and in Kiev, Ukraine. Thanks to help of our colleagues, the texts were greatly improved.

The editors dedicate this book to Professor David Gaunt, who initiated and lead the project. Officially, David retired in fall 2011, but has carried on breaking new ground, taking on new scientific challenges in the field of genocide studies. As David's former PhD students, Andrej Kotljarchuk (one of the contributing authors) and Piotr Wawrzeniuk (one of the editors and contributing authors) take this opportunity to honor their Professor, who during their studies proved to be an inspiring, erudite and very patient supervisor.

Notes

In this book, the Library of Congress system for the Romanization of Cyrillic letters has been used. However, there have been a few modifications. The soft sign ('ь') transcription has been left out. The ligatures in the Romanization of 'й', 'ж', 'ц', 'я', 'ю' and 'є' have not been used.

Various Russian names frequently used in the texts and footnotes are also written in their Anglicized plural versions, for example, desiatinas, sazhens.

In the book, the names of historical towns founded during the imperial period are written in Russian such as Ekaterinoslav, Odessa etc., as source material of imperial origin has been used. For instance, the name of the colony of Khortytsia (Ukrainian) is written in the version found in the source material – Khortitsia (Russian). However, the names of the rivers are written in Ukrainian (Pivdennyi Buh and Dnipro). Some generally used geographical names are used, such as Crimea and Zaporizhian Sich. When the question comes to the administration, the ambition has been to use era-typical names.

In the references to the source material, Russian or Ukrainian names are used depending on whether the material has been prepared and structured in Russian or Ukrainian. This explains the differences in the end notes of Svitlana Bobyleva who uses material from the imperial period, and Andrej Kotljarchuk who mainly uses documents originating from Ukrainian SSR, for instance.

The names of institutions and documents (journals, newspapers etc.) are first written in the original language, and then followed by translation in to English in brackets.

The documents cited in this volume have been translated into English by the respective authors, or by the editors.

Geographical Names

Historical name	Current name
Chernigov	Chernihiv, Chernihiv Oblast (Ukraine)
Dagö	Hiiumaa (Estonia)
Danzig	Gdańsk (Poland)
Ekaterinoslav	Dnipropetrovsk, Dnipropetrovsk Oblast (Ukraine)
Gammalsvenskby	(in Ukrainian: Staroshvedske; in Russian: Staroshvedskoe; in English: Old-Swedish Village; in German: Alt-Schwedendorf) Zmiivka, Kherson Oblast (Ukraine)
Kakhovka	Kakhovka, Kherson Oblast (Ukraine)
Kaluga	Kaluga, Kaluga Oblast (Russian Federation)
Kazykermen (Berislav)	Beryslav, Kherson Oblast (Ukraine)
Khortitsa	Khortytsia, Zaporizhzhia Oblast (Ukraine)
Kursk	Kursk, Kursk Oblast (Russian Federation)
Priazove	Pryazovia, Azov Sea territories (Ukraine)
Prichernomore	Prychornomoria, Black Sea territories (Ukraine)
Pridnestrove	Pridnestrove, Dniester River territories (Moldova)
Reshetilovka	Reshetylivka, Poltava Oblast (Ukraine)
Reval	Tallinn (Estonia)
Tambov	Tambov, Tambov Oblast (Russian Federation)
Tula	Tula, Tula Oblast (Russian Federation)
Åbo/Turku	Åbo/Turku (Finland)

Abbreviations

ARAB	Arbetarrörelsens arkiv och bibliotek (Labour Movement Archives and Library) Stockholm, Sweden
DADO	Derzhavnyi arkhiv Dnipropetrovskoi oblasti (State Archives of Dnipropetrovsk Oblast) Dnipropetrovsk, Ukraine
DAKhO	Derzhavnyi arkhiv Khersonskoi oblasti (State Archives of Kherson Oblast) Kherson, Ukraine
DAOO	Derzhavnyi arkhiv Odeskoi oblasti (State Archives of Odesa Oblast) Odesa, Ukraine
DGU	Dnipropetrovskii gosudarstvennyi universitet (Dnipropetrovsk State University) Dnipropetrovsk, Ukraine

KhDU	Khersonskyi derzhavnyi universytet (Kherson State University) Kherson, Ukraine
PSZRI	Polnoe sobranie zakonov Rossiiskoi imperii (Complete Collection of Laws of the Russian Empire)
RA	Riksarkivet (The National Archives) Stockholm, Sweden
RGASPI	Rossiiskii Gosudarstvennyi archiv sotsialno-politicheskoi istorii (Russian State Archive for Social and Political History) Moscow, Russia
RGIA	Rossiiskii Gosudarstvennyi istoricheskii archiv (Russian State Historical Archives) St Petersburg, Russia
TsKNM	Tsentralnyi Komitet natsionalnykh menshinstv (Central Committee for the National Minorities) Moscow, Russia
ECCI	Executive Committee of the Comintern
SKP	Sveriges Kommunistiska Parti (Swedish Communist Party)
VKP(b)	Vsesoiuznaia Kommunisticheskaia Partiia (bolshevikov) (All - Union Communist Party (Bolsheviks)
TASS	Telegrafnoe agenstvo Sovetskogo Soiuza (Telegraph Agency of the Soviet Union)
KMA	Kvinnliga Missions Arbetare (Female Missionary Workers)
GPU	Gosudarstvennoe politicheskoe upravlenie (The State Political Directorate)
NKVD	Narodnyi Komissariat Vnutrennikh Del (The People's Commissariat for Internal Affairs)
TsK VKP (b)	Tsentralnyi Komitet Vsesoiuznoi Kommunisticheskoi Partii (bolshevikov) (Central Committee of All-Union Communist Party (Bolsheviks)
RGAKFD	Rossiiskii gosudarstvennyi arkhiv kinofotodokumentov (The Russian State Documentary Film and Photo Archive at Krasnogorsk)
TsDAGO	Tsentralnyi derzhavnyi arkhiv hromadskykh obiednan Ukrainy (Central State Archives of the Public Organizations of Ukraine)
SLS FS	Svenska litteratursällskapet i Finland, Folkkulturarkivet och språkarkivet (Swedish Literature Society in Finland, Archives of folkore and language)
SLS HLA	Svenska litteratursällskapet i Finland, Historiska och litteraturhistoriska arkivet (Swedish Literature Society in Finland, Archives of History and Literature), stored at the National Library of Finland

Archival and bibliography terms

f.	fond (holding)
op.	opis, opys (register)
d.	delo (file)
ch.	chast/chastyna (part)
l.	list (page)
ll.	listy (pages)
sobr.	sobranie (collection)
str.	stranitsa, storinka (page)
t.	tom (volume)
spr.	sprava (file)
ark.	arkush (page)
arkk.	arkushi (pages)
vyp.	vypusk (issue)
kn.	kniga/knyga (book)
pril.	prilozhenie (appendix)

Map 1: Before New Russia. The territory of the future Russian province in 1745, while a part of the Khanate of Crimea. *Tataria Minor cum Adiacentibus Kiovensi et Belgorodensi Guberniis*, 1745, Krigsarkivet 0403/31/A/007h.

Previous page: **Map 2:** "Empty" space to be populated? New Russia in 1779, waiting to be colonized. The Crimea to the south remained under Tatar rule for another four years. *Mappa Generalis Gubernii Novae Russiae in Circulos Divisi 1779 Suctore*, Krigsarkivet 0403/33/020 1.

Map 3: Dagö, the home island of the ancestors of Gammalsvenskby Swedes, 1802. *Der Hapsalsche Kreis,* Krigsarkivet 0043/32/067.

Approaching the "Lost Swedish Tribe" in Ukraine

PIOTR WAWRZENIUK & JULIA MALITSKA

Tracing the "lost tribe"
– Gammalsvenskby as a research problem

In the spring of 1782 a group of villagers of Swedish origin reached their destination on the right bank of Dnipro River, about fifty kilometers from the centre of Kherson Oblast in Ukraine of today. Tradition has it that they celebrated mass, thanking the Heavens for their arrival at their destination. The Swedes had made their way to Ukraine from the remote island of Dagö (Hiiumaa) on the coast of the Duchy of Estonia. These villagers were in the vanguard of the colonization of the steppes bordering the Black Sea, an area Russia conquered in the 1770s. The village founded on the very spot where their journey ended, became known as "Gammalsvenskby" by its inhabitants (from the Russian "Staroshvedskoe," literally meaning "Old Swedish Village"). The village remained largely intact until 1929, when a majority of the villagers decided to leave for Sweden. This book covers the developments from the planning of the southbound journey from Dagö in 1781 to the aftermath of the migration to Sweden.

When the research project about Gammalsvenskby was under development, the main question concerned what seemed to be a highly detailed nation-building process within a small group of peasants of Swedish origin. Living in southern Russia, and lacking the elites frequently viewed as crucial for such a process to succeed, the inhabitants of Gammalsvenskby seemed to manage their Swedish ancestry inexplicably well during a century and a half. However, once the project team, consisting of researchers from Södertörn University (Sweden) and Dnipropetrovsk National University (Ukraine), began to study various aspects of the history of the village, it transpired that the processes that took place in Gammalsvenskby were not as straightforward as previously described. There were institutions and individuals that had a tremendous impact on the course of events. To the members of the team, the history of the village ceased to be that which it had traditionally been depicted as – a history of a handful of people, Swedish patriots, displaced from their original habitat by a cruel destiny, and defending their culture against all odds in hostile surroundings. Therefore, the main intention of the project was to employ new empirical material, put forward new questions, and by that offer new perspectives on the history of Gammalsvenskby.

The abundance of unused source material directed our work towards bringing its contents to the readership rather than contributing with theoretical approaches to the fields of migration studies and social history. The possible future directions of continued research on the subject suggest that theoretical concepts of ethnicity, nation and nationalism, along with comparisons with other groups who have experienced a similar fate, may contribute to the general understanding of the processes that the population of Gammalsvenskby went through from the end of the eighteenth century up to the start of the Second World War.[1]

The members of the project thus raised questions as to the character of the migration of the Swedes, their adaptation to the physical milieu of the steppes, and their relationship with the state administration and various groups that populated the area. Finally, the implications of the political context in Russia, Finland, Sweden and the USSR for the development of the village would be studied. Earlier research has shown that such processes and relations alter the group and self-identity, depending on the degree of exposure to the new environment, the cultural distance between the culture of the immigrants and that of their new location, the immigrants' ability to maintain contact with their original culture, and their sentiments towards the new culture.[2]

---

[1] Charlotta Hillerdal, *People in Between. Ethnicity and Material Identity, a New Approach to Deconstructed Concepts* (Uppsala: Uppsala University, 2009). Unfortunately, Hillerdal fails to successfully apply the very concepts she suggests, making her approach both unhistorical and anachronistic, and the final result questionable.

[2] Tinghög, Petter, *Migration, Stress and Mental Ill Health: Postmigration Factors and the Experiences in the Swedish Context* (Linköping: Linköping University. Faculty of Arts and Science, 2009), 14.

Although obviously devoid of miracles, the history of Gammalsvenskby contains several interesting turns. From the beginning of the migration in 1781 to the Stalinist repression in the 1930s, this book offers a study of broad-reaching processes and developments by looking into the situation of a small group of people. Conversely, the history of the village sheds considerable light on the developments in Russia, the Soviet Union, Sweden and Finland. Contained is a combination of micro and macro history, where particular features prove helpful in explaining something general, and vice versa. The processes that had great impact on the village's population can be summarized in two words – migration and modernization.

It has been claimed that "to study the European history is to study migration."[3] At least on three occasions – in 1781, 1929 and 1931 – the entire population of the village or a considerable portion decided to seek a better life and start over elsewhere. In 1781, the then Dagö islanders migrated to the steppes, and the village that would become Gammalsvenskby was born. In 1929, the majority of the population moved to Sweden following large-scale lobbying by the villagers and their backers in Sweden. Only two years later, a group of former villagers who were dissatisfied with the conditions offered by the Swedish authorities, and who found it difficult adapting to Swedish society, decided to move back to what then was the Ukrainian Soviet Republic, a step stimulated by intense Communist campaigning among the group. As migration studies show, a group's reluctance to move is usually eased by earlier experiences and memories of having migrated. A group of discontented villagers who did not wish to move back to the USSR migrated to Canada in 1931. Long before that, several families from Gammalsvenskby had migrated to Canada and Siberia in the 1880s and 1890s. Most of the few remaining Dagö Swedes left the island in 1941.

Embedded in the history of the village are two grand top-down modernization projects – the Russian one, originating in the times of Catherine II, and the Soviet one, carried out in the early 1920s. The former was driven from a physiocratic standpoint, where access to arable land and its cultivation were seen as the base of wealth and prosperity, and the conviction that an influx of migrants from Central Europe would automatically result in the swift improvement of

---

[3] Menz, Georg, *The Political Economy of Managed Migration* (Oxford: Oxford University Press, 2008), 1.

agricultural methods and yields, and the development of handicrafts and manufacturing.[4] On the most general level, the Soviet project was viewed by its architects as addressing and mending the shortcomings and failures of the imperial colonization and agriculture policy by creating a new peasant class, modernized collective agriculture and finally – the Communist society. Caught in the midst of these two projects were the residents of Gammalsvenskby, who suffered demographic losses on both occasions. Once in place in 1782, the villagers went through a difficult trial-and-error learning process which is closely described in three of the four articles of this volume. The migration to southern Russia also saw the population of the village face and deal with the phenomena of modernization such as improving communications and swift access to regional and international markets.

To a lesser degree, but still very concretely so, the villagers were subjected to Swedish influence after sustainable links with Sweden were established in the 1880s. In frequent contact with Sweden and the Swedophones in Finland, the villagers faced Swedish and Finnish dilemmas of cultural and political differentiation, features that, along with several others, have been described as characteristic of modernization.[5] The visitors from Scandinavia brought with them convictions that were formed by the specific political and cultural context in the home countries. Those convictions constituted the prism through which the village was presented. Naturally, this way of viewing the course of events in Gammalsvenskby did not take into account the historical development of the village, and often proved inaccurate.

Colonization of the Black Sea steppe and imperial policies in the region

Russia's colonization and incorporation of the steppe reflected and produced a particularly complicated kind of imperialism, one in which empire building, state building, society building, and nation building intertwined.[6] The steppe as a whole was never described as a colony,

---

[4] From a vast amount of literature one finds a good overview in Duran, James A Jr., "Catherine II, Potemkin, and Colonization Policy in Southern Russia," *Russian Review*, Vol. 28, No. 1 (Jan., 1969), p. 23. For a detailed account, see the remaining part of the same article and the texts of Bobyleva och Malitska in this volume.
[5] Sejersted, Francis, *Socialdemokratins tidsålder: Sverige och Norge under 1900-talet* (Lund 2005: Nya Doxa).
[6] Willard Sunderland, *Taming the Wild Field: Colonization and Empire on the Russian Steppe.* (Cornell University, 2004), 5.

presumably because it was not geographically separated from the rest of the state, although in other respects – most obviously, the name New Russia – the colonial status seemed clear. By the dawn of the twentieth century, the steppe had been so profoundly transformed by Russian imperialism that it was difficult for contemporaries to determine whether it constituted a borderland, a colony, or Russia itself.[7] The view of colonization as a popular, natural, and mostly gentle movement that unfolded within an empire, but was not itself imperialist, was the product of myth, of wishful thinking by the Russian elite. There were no natural barriers between the steppe and "Russia," the region was rather close to the center of the empire, there seemed to be an abundant supply of "open" land suitable for farming or stock raising, there was no state organization there and the indigenous population was sparse. All this combined to make Russian migration to the south a relatively simple undertaking which could easily be interpreted as an elemental, organic process.[8]

A considerable proportion of those who colonized New Russia were Russian and Ukrainian peasants but foreigners also contributed to shaping the region.

The aims of the Russian government were partly economic. By encouraging foreign settlements the government hoped to be able to develop lands that had so far been uninhabited and thus increase revenues, to improve the balance of trade and to ease rural over-population in central Russia. There were also political goals such as improving border security, strengthening Russian authority, and populating the new territories with loyal peoples. The foreigners were considered to be of superior virtues compared to the autochthonous population. Thus, they were expected to carry out "cultural" and "civilizing" missions and elevate the remaining population by example. These tasks were connected with the economic one – the promotion of new methods of production among other groups of the population in the colonized territories.

In the eighteenth century, serfdom in central Russia deprived the Russian peasantry of free movement, preventing any substantial mobility into the territory that was being colonized. The internal demographic potential of the Russian Empire was, therefore, insufficient

---

[7] Sunderland, *Taming the Wild Field*, 89, 223.
[8] Sunderland, *Taming the Wild Field*, 226–227.

to fulfill the government's colonization plans. The peasants were legally tied to territories already under cultivation. While not denying the native population the possibility to take part in the mastering and opening up of the new incorporated territories, Russia's government turned to the Central European population.

The new phase of Russia's colonization policy on the steppe was introduced as a result of large-scale territorial expansion in the second half of the eighteenth century. The recently annexed, nomadic-populated or scarcely populated lands (Caucasus and Volga regions etc.), were to be absorbed and gradually integrated into the imperial space. The victories in the wars against Turkey in 1768–1774, 1787–1791 and Count Grigorii Potemkin's activities, directed part of the colonization to the new acquisitions of the so-called Southern Russia or New Russia.[9] As a result of the strengthening of Russian influence in the Black Sea region after the peace treaty with Turkey in 1774 and the gradual advancement of Russia's borders to the south, the Zaporizhian Sich had lost its main function of being a Russian outpost against the Turks and Tatars. Considering the Sich to be a rebellious centre of aristocratic struggle, Catherine II abolished it in 1775. The lands of the former Zaporizhian Sich and the Cossack Hetmanate, along with the territories between the Pivdennyi Buh and Dnipro rivers, were included in the state fund for land distribution.[10]

The territorial-administrative absorption of the Azov and Black Sea territories went hand in hand with the colonization process. In 1764, the province of New Russia was founded and it existed until 1775. Count Grigorii Potemkin was appointed its governor-general.[11] After the abolition of the Zaporizhian Sich in 1775, its lands were attached to the

---

[9] *Rossiia. Polnoe geograficheskoe opisanie nashego otechestva,* ed. Petr Semenov-Tian-Shanskii, t.14. Novorossiia i Krym (Sankt-Petersburg: Izd-vo A. F. Devrieva, 1910), 157–161; John P. LeDonne, *The Russian Empire and the World, 1700–1917: the Geopolitics of Expansion and Containment* (New York: Oxford Univ. Press, 1997), 43–62; Andreas Kappeler, *Rossiia iak polietnichna derzhava: Vynyknennia. Istoriia. Rozpad* (Lviv: Vydavnytstvo Ukrainskogo Katolytskogo universytetu, 2005), 62–70; Evgenii Zagorovskii, *Inostrannaia kolonizatsiia Novorossii v 18 veke* (Odessa: Tsentr. Tip. S. Rozenshtraukha i N. Lemberga, 1913), 2.

[10] Andreas Kappeler, *Rossiia iak polietnichna derzhava,* 42–45; Elena Druzhynina, *Severnoe Prichernomore v 1775–1800* (Moskva: Nauka, 1959), 52–53; *Voenno-statisticheskoe obozrenie Rossiiskoi imperii,* t. 11, ch. 1. Khersonskaia guberniia (Sankt-Petersburg: Tip. Departementa Gen. Shtaba, 1849), 82.

[11] Natalia Shushliannikova, *Rozpovidi z istorii Khersonskogo kraiu* (Kherson: KhDU, 2003), 6.

New Russia and Azov provinces, which were made up of the former New Russia Province and the lands of the Don Cossacks.[12] In 1784, the next large administrative-territorial changes took place: the New Russia and the Azov provinces formed Ekaterinoslav viceroyalty. Additionally, the Senate proclaimed a nominal decree founding the Tavriia region on the territory of the former Crimean khanate.[13] In 1796 the districts of Kerch, Kinburn and Enikale, Crimea and a considerable area between Pivdennyi Buh and Dniester rivers, together with the lands of the former Zaporizhian Sich, formed the New Russia province which in 1803 was divided into three provinces: Ekaterinoslav, Kherson and Tavriia.[14]

The colonization of the Black Sea territory was to some extent spontaneous and to some extent organized by the Russian state. Russia had vast territories to the east and south opened to settlement. When these territories were opened to settlers, the Russian government could benefit from the experience of other European countries (particularly Prussia) in controlling, occupying and populating new territories. On 4 December 1762 Catherine II issued a Manifesto inviting foreigners to settle in Russia.[15] The purpose was twofold. The first aim was to encourage cultivation of the vast steppes and develop mining, commerce, and manufacturing. This was the reasoning presented in the manifesto. The second aim was the development of land in a region where minor, but protracted military problems were experienced along the southern frontiers. New settlements would provide a buffer zone between the peasant population of Russia and its nomadic neighbors. However, the number of artisans who came to settle in the region was small, and the manifesto was generally not considered to have achieved its goal.

Therefore, Catherine II issued a new document on 22 July 1763, offering more attractive privileges for newcomers. Travel expenses would

---

[12] *Voenno-statisticheskoe obozrenie Rossiiskoi imperii*. t. 11, ch. 1. Khersonskaia guberniia (Sankt-Petersburg: Tip. Departementa Gen. Shtaba, 1849), 82; Elena Druzhynina, *Severnoe Prichernomore v 1775-1800*, 49-53.

[13] Rasporiazheniia svetleishego Grigoriia Aleksandrovicha Potemkina-Tavricheskogo kasatelno ustroeniia Tavricheskoi oblasti s 1781 po 1786-i god, in *Zapiski imperatorskogo Odesskogo obshchestva istorii i drevnostei*, t.12 (Odessa: Franko-rus. tip. L. Danikana, 1881), 322-323; *Rossiia*, ed. Petr Semenov-Tian'-Shanskii, t. 14, 161-162; Elena Druzhynina, *Severnoe Prichernomore*, 57; Vladimir Kabuzan, *Zaselenie Novorossii (Ekaterinoslavskoi i Khersonskoi gubernii) v 18 – pervoi polovine 19 vv. (1719-1858)* (Moskva: Nauka, 1976), 93.

[14] Shushliannikova, *Rozpovidi z istorii Khersonskogo krau*, 8.

[15] *Nemtsy-kolonisty v vek Ekateriny*, ed. Elena Lykova, M. Osekina (Moskva: "Drevlekhranilishche," 2004), 10-11.

be paid for by the Russian state for those who could not afford the journey; free land was granted for tillage in certain areas, primarily in the Volga River region; and religious freedom would be granted to the incoming Christian population. The colonists were not allowed to convert the Orthodox population, but were free to proselytize among Muslims. The settlers on uncultivated territory would also be granted freedom from taxes and tributes for thirty years. In addition, tradesmen who settled in the towns would be free from taxes for a period of between five and ten years depending on the location. The colonists would be granted free lodging for the initial six months of settlement, and receive interest free loans for the construction of houses and purchasing of farm equipment and cattle. The loans would be repayable only after ten years. The newcomers would receive the right to self-government of separately established colonies and freedom from import duties on all goods they brought with them. They were granted inducements for the manufacturing of goods, and freedom from military service.[16] In fact, the government passed the task of building a social and economic structure in the colonized areas from scratch on to the newcomers.

With these new enticements in hand, Russian representatives and government agents actively began to recruit immigrants abroad. For various reasons, non-German populations did not respond well. Some countries that allowed free publication of the invitation were already enjoying relative prosperity and had their own overseas colonies. For example, an English-speaking colony in America would be more attractive to an Englishman than the strange and remote land of Russia. Muslims from Turkish lands foresaw their enserfment by the Russians. The Habsburg Empire forbade emigration after it reached high levels in 1760s, and because of their own settlement programs in the Hungarian territory.[17] Active recruitment could only take place in free cities and states where there were no laws limiting emigration.

Several German states were unable to control migration, which reached particularly high levels in the Kingdom of Prussia including Silesia and Pomerania; Württemberg; Bohemia; the Grand Duchies of Baden and Hessen; the cities of Lübeck, Danzig and Mainz on the Rhine. The typical reasons for migration – then as now – were war, displacement caused by war, to avoid compulsory military service; dangers

---

[16] *Nemtsy v istorii Rossii: dokumenty vysshykh organov vlasti i voennogo komandovaniia, 1652–1917*, ed. Viktor Diesendorf (Moskva: MFD: Materik, 2006), 23–27.
[17] Zagorovskii, *Inostrannaia kolonizatsiia Novorossii*, 3.

posed by climatic and geographical conditions (flooding, drought); political oppression or religious persecution; a friend or relative who was encouraging migration; and possibilities to receive employment or improve one's economic situation. Among the reasons for migration, one should also mention avoiding being drafted and the high taxes exacted by the German states, long-term lease of men as mercenaries to America; stern management methods; the Seven Years' War (1756–1763) and the French Revolutionary and Napoleonic Wars (1792–1815), along with foreign occupation and other military conflicts. Political instability, poor harvests and lean years, epidemics of plague and cholera caused a new wave of migration from the European states in the eighteenth century.[18]

The scale of migration caused radical changes in the ethnic structure of the settlers and pushed the Russian government to search for new "human capital". Russian and Ukrainian peasants played a significant role in the colonization and the economic mastering of the Azov and Black Sea territories. New settlers came from the Central Russian provinces, the left bank Ukraine, and Bessarabia.[19] Since the second half of the eighteenth century, people from foreign countries began to play a considerable role in the colonization of this territory. The edict of Joseph II from 1768, forbidding migration from the Habsburg lands, did not stop the human flow from Europe; it only changed its source.

All ethnic groups that moved to uncultivated new lands were granted privileges, but the conditions of colonization were unique for each group. They determined not only the differentiation in the normative granting of land, but also civil rights and social liberties. Russians and Ukrainians, and Orthodox peasants in general, were given minimal social and economic privileges compared to the foreign settlers.[20]

It was only natural that the government should wish to attract people from ethnic groups that lived near the state border: Bulgarians, Poles, Jews, Moldavians, and Germans. However, the settlement of other

[18] Svetlana Bobyleva, "Prichiny migratsii nemetskogo naseleniia na Ukrainu v 18- pervoi polovine 19 v.," in *Voprosy germanskoi istorii: ukrainsko-nemetskie sviazi v novoe i noveishee vremia*, ed. Sergei Plokhii (Dnipropetrovsk: DGU, 1995), 30–41.
[19] Iaroslav Boiko, Nataliia Danylenko, "Formuvannia etnichnogo skladu naselennia Pivdennoi Ukrainy (kinets 19–20st.)," *Ukrainskyi istorychnyi zhurnal*, no. 9 (1992), 54–65; Sergei Bruk, Vladimir Kabuzan, "Migratsiia naseleniia v Rossii v 18-nachale 20 vv. (chislennost, struktura, geografiia)," *Istoriia SSSR*, no. 4 (1984), 41–59.
[20] Alexander Klaus, *Nashi kolonii. Opyt i materialy po istorii i statistike inostrannoi kolonizatsii v Rossii, vyp. 1* (St Petersburg: Tip. V.V. Nusval'ta, 1869), 21.

foreign groups (such as Italians and Swedes) was a result of unexpected developments that the authorities were quick to realize. This fact considerably determined the impact of each group on the socio-cultural and economic development of the southern provinces of imperial Russia. By offering land and various privileges to the foreign settlers, the Russian government aimed to create faithful and loyal subjects, quite unlike the unruly Zaporizhian Cossacks. Depending on time and place, the colonization process could be hesitant or intense; "popular" or "state-directed"; Russian, foreign, "alien", or "sectarian."[21]

The government was eager to involve as many settlers as possible, particularly so after the Habsburg lands were closed for emigration. The first phase of colonization was ambiguous. On the one hand, by mastering the enormous territories of virgin lands, opening new factories and inventing new agricultural tools, colonists had a considerable impact on the economic development of these lands. On the other hand, if the Zaporizhian Cossacks, who were already accustomed to the local conditions, had not been forced to leave their native lands but had been granted the same privileges as the colonists, the results would probably have been even more beneficial. While not denying the positive influence of the colonists, it should be noted that many of them were incapable of physical work, let alone grasp the proportions of their tasks during Catherine II's and Paul I's colonization era. Only after 1804, when the new Tsar, Alexander I, extended another invitation to settle in this region, did the structure of the colonists change. However, because of the shortage of available lands his invitation was made more specific and selective than Catherine's. He sought people who were particularly skilled in agriculture and handicrafts – well-to-do farmers with skills in viticulture, management and the breeding of livestock. While they received some financial and logistic assistance with their relocation, they were also expected to bring with them significant quantities of cash and goods. Since the introduction of explicit rules for the reception and the settling down of colonists in February 1804, colonist status could be attained only by settlers with families, who possessed a certain amount of capital, were well-behaved and could be considered useful to the country such as farmers cattle-breeders, gardeners, wine-makers, and artisans.[22]

---

[21] Sunderland, *Taming the Wild Field*, 223.
[22] *Nemtsy v istorii Rossii*, Diesendorf, 144–147.

As more and more of the steppe was absorbed, as the ambitions of the government increased, the bureaucratic machinery also grew.[23] In 1763, the Office for Foreigners' Guardianship (*Kantseliariia opekunstva inostrannykh*) was established in St Petersburg under the management of Catherine II's favorite Grigorii Orlov. It had the same powers as a State Board and an annual budget of 20,000 rubles. In 1782 after the formation of the provinces, that office was abolished and the management of the colonists and state peasants was brought under the supervision of *Direktora domovodstva*. Despite the large sums spent by the state to attract foreigners and to settle them, there were colonies which suffered extreme decline and many general complaints came from the settlers. For that reason, a new board was set up in 1797 to manage the colonies: the Board of State Economy, Guardianship of Foreigners and Rural Husbandry (*Ekspeditsiia gosudarstvennogo khoziaistva opekunstva inostrannykh i selskogo domovodstva*, from now on referred to as "the Board." In 1802 it was attached to the Ministry of Internal Affairs but was abolished shortly after.

The Board introduced auditing inspections in order to get a clear picture of the settlers' living conditions and the reasons for the unsatisfactory development of the colonies. Officials were sent to the colonies all over the country and obliged to acquaint themselves with the colonists' lives and agricultural activities. Thus, Court Adviser Samuel Contenius (1749–1830), an official of the Geographical department, was sent to New Russia to inspect the foreign settlements in 1798–1800. He was ordered to personally investigate the settlers' economic activities in detail, identify their shortcomings, and submit an account of his findings.

Having conducted this inspection, Contenius blamed the government for the deplorable economic situation of the New Russia colonists.[24] In his report to the Senate, he listed the following obstacles: insufficient development of animal husbandry because of drought, poor harvests, and parasites; shortage of agricultural tools; permanent cattle disease; poor mastering of the crafts, mainly during winter times; the colonists disobeyed the orders of the local government.[25] To

---

[23] Sunderland, *Taming the Wild Field*, 97–136.
[24] Alexander Velitsyn, *Nemtsy v Rossii. Ocherki nemetskoi kolonizatsii na Iuge i Vostoke Rossii* (Sankt-Peterburg: "Obshchestvennaia polza," 1893), 93.
[25] *Samuil Khristianovich Contenius ob inostrannoi kolonizatsii Iuzhnoi Rossii, sbornik dokumentov 1801–1829*, ed. Olga Eisfeld (Odessa: Astroprint, 2003), 42–45.

alleviate this, he suggested the government write off the debts and allot more land to the colonists.[26]

The establishment in 1800 of the Guardianship Office for New Russia Foreign Settlers of Southern Russia (*Kontora opekunstva Novorossiiskikh inostrannykh poselentsev Iuzhnogo kraia Rossii*)[27] headed by Samuel Contenius and the subsequent restructuring of the management of the colonies was a powerful step towards more efficient governmental support and supervision of the foreign colonists.[28]

In 1818 the management of the foreign colonies was reorganized again as the number of colonists had increased considerably. An imperial decree introduced the Trustees Committee for Foreign Settlers in Southern Russia (*Popechitelnyi komitet inostrannykh poselentsev Iuzhnogo kraia Rossii*)[29] consisting of the Ekaterinoslav, Odessa and Bessarabia Guardianship Offices.[30] Its abolishment in 1833 marked the end of the period of foreign colonists' settlement and their migration into the Russian Empire. Consequently, in 1837 the colonists were placed under the supervision of the Ministry of State Property and there was no longer a separate administration for the colonists.[31] Moreover, starting from the 1830s, government policy took a new turn. A new ideology came into being involving the encouragement of an "official nationality" based on the principles of Orthodoxy, autocracy, Nationality and Slavdom. This ideology itself was a call for "constructing" an identity that would exclude non-Orthodox or culturally non-conformist elements.[32] Eventually, foreign colonists were perceived as a potential threat to Russian national identity, unless they converted to Orthodox Christianity.

The unique legal status of the colonists in Russian society prevented their rapid assimilation with the rest of the population. Expectations of the Russian government that the colonists not only would colonize the unsettled lands, but also, in a certain way, stimulate a long-lasting develop-

---

[26] DADO, f. 134, op.1, spr. 28, 33.
[27] Abbreviated as: the Guardianship Office.
[28] *Nemtsy v istorii Rossii*, Diesendorf, 81–95.
[29] Abbreviated as: the Trustees Committee.
[30] *Nemtsy v istorii Rossii*, Diesendorf, 190–194.
[31] *Ocherki istorii nemtsev i mennonitov Iuga Ukrainy (konets 18– pervaia polovina 19 vekov)*, ed. Svetlana Bobyleva (Dnipropetrovsk: Art-press, 1999), 58–59.
[32] Sergei I. Zhuk, *Russia's Lost Reformation: Peasants, Millennialism, and Radical Sects in Southern Russia and Ukraine, 1830-1917* (Woodrow Wilson Center Press, 2004), 35; James Urry, "Mennonites, Nationalism and the State in Imperial Russia," in *Journal of Mennonite Studies*, vol.12 (1994), 69–71.

ment of agriculture and modernization of southern Russia were not fully realized. During almost all of the nineteenth century, the effect the colonists had on the economy differed only slightly from that of Russian peasant households. However, the colonists constantly improved agricultural tools and introduced new agricultural machines and crops. Still, foreign settlers did not make a deep impact on their next-door neighbors due to the isolation of the colonist societies, their legal separation from the rest of the rural population, and the cultural, and mental distance between the Russian and Ukrainian peasants and the colonists. Moreover, the improved agricultural tools remained unattainable for the Ukrainian and Russian peasants, because of their relative poverty.[33] Owing to their lack of knowledge of Russian, their economic self-sufficiency and self-governance, their religious creed and ethos, the colonists remained separated from their Ukrainian and Russian neighbors.

The second half of the nineteenth century was a period of rapid socio-economic development in Russia. A number of so-called "bourgeois" reforms (land, administrative, judicial, educational and military reforms) were introduced and with them came profound changes in the governmental attitude and official discourse towards the foreign colonists. Alexander II's decree of 4 July 1871 embodied "great changes" for the colonists. The decree abolished the privileges of the colonists, i.e. colonist status and the special management of the colonies. Foreign colonists were put under common Russian governmental rule and received the status of landowner-settler (*sobstvennik-poselianin*) with rights and duties equivalent to the state peasants after the emancipation in 1861.[34] Further foundation of colonies, after 1872 – the settlements of settler-owners, could take place on state lands, but also on other land purchased by colonists. The introduction of general military service in 1874 extended to the colonists as well. This was one of the main reasons for Mennonite emigration to Canada and the USA. In the second half of the nineteenth century, a series of "questions" occupied a prominent place in the Russian political lexicon. While some questions concerned political and social issues across the empire as a whole, others, such as the Jewish question,

---

[33] Elvira Plesskaia, "Problemy sokhraneniia natsionalnoi kultury v usloviiakh sushchestvovaniia i vzaimodeistviia s kulturoi titulnoi natsii," in *Kliuchevye problemy istorii rossiiskikh nemtsev* (Moskva: MSNK-press, 2004), 194–197; L. G. Friesen. "Bukkers, Plows and Lobogreikas: Peasant Acquisition of Agricultural Implements in Russia before 1900," in *Russian Review*, vol. 53, no. 3 (1994), 399–418.

[34] *Nemtsy v istorii Rossii*, ed. Diesendorf, 507–516.

the Ukrainian question, and the Baltic question pertained only to non-Russian subjects of the empire.[35] Moreover, by the 1870s the "German element" as a whole had become problematic enough to be labeled a "question" – the so-called "German question". Purchases of land by German colonist were in turn perceived as a "threat".[36] Gradually, formal Russification and informal Russianisation took place all over the foreign settlements of the Russian Empire.[37]

The end of the nineteenth and the early twentieth century saw a crisis of agriculture throughout the country. Ex-colonists lost land and, as a result, emigration grew. Because of Prime Minister Peter Stolypin's agrarian reforms 1907–1914, most of the ex-colonists became private owners of their land.[38] However, many landless peasants or peasants who had had insufficient land migrated to Siberia. In October 1914, the Minister for Internal Affairs sent a secret circular in which he urgently recommended that settlements and districts with German names instead be given Russian names.[39] It was soon implemented.

A central aspect of Russia's participation in the First World War was a sweeping campaign against so-called "enemy aliens" in order to mobilize better for war. Not only ethnic Germans but also Jews, Muslims, Czechs, Poles, Slovaks, Bulgarians, Greeks, and Serbs were included among the "enemy subjects." The popular campaign quickly expanded well beyond enemy subjects to affect large numbers of naturalized immigrants and Russian citizens whose loyalty was questioned because of their ethnicity, religion, or former citizenship.[40] A similar campaign, but with a more paranoid touch and hundreds of thousands of victims, was conducted under Stalin in the second half of 1930s. It was directed against several minority groups primarily in the western borderlands. Poles and Germans turned out to be the campaign's main targets, but it also reached the Swedes in Gammalsvenskby.[41]

---

[35] Elena Campbell, *Russian Empire: Space, People, Power 1700–1930*, p. 320.
[36] Sunderland, *Taming the Wild Field*, 189.
[37] *Nemtsy v istorii Rossii*, Diesendorf, 551–552, 555–556; James Urry, "Mennonites, Nationalism and the State in Imperial Russia," in *Journal of Mennonite Studies*, vol.12 (1994), 65–88.
[38] Eric Lohr, *Nationalizing the Russian Empire: The Campaign against Enemy Aliens during World War I* (Harvard University Press, 2003), 90–91.
[39] *Nemtsy v istorii Rossii*, Diesendorf, 558–560.
[40] Lohr, *Nationalizing the Russian Empire*, 1–9, 109-111,166–173.
[41] See Kotljarchuk's article in this volume.

However, wartime hostility focused predominantly on people of "German origin" as they had grown into a population of over two million by the 1897 census.⁴² According to the "liquidation laws" 1914–1917 German meetings, along with the use of, and teaching in, the German language were forbidden. Restrictions on German ownership of land and land tenure were introduced; first in the western borderlands, then all over the country.⁴³ Germans were moved from the proximity of the war-front territory. Finally, a special committee for the fight against German dominance was established.⁴⁴

The campaign resulted in the forced migration of roughly one million civilians, nationalization of a substantial portion of the economy, and the transfer of extensive land holdings and rural properties from the targeted minorities to groups favored by the state.⁴⁵ Such a campaign had a direct impact on the multinational society of New Russia as its aim was the creation of a homogenous nation state and the leveling of the legal and cultural differences between the socioeconomic and ethnic groups of the population.

From the second half of the eighteenth century until the First World War, Russia's colonization policy in the Azov and Black Sea region and official attitudes towards the colonists went through a far-ranging evolution.⁴⁶ From the utopian expectations of the modernizing "mission" of the colonists, the attitude changed into deep suspicion with dystopian undertones. The modernizing goals that encompassed the large-scale economic and social reshaping of the southern outskirts of the empire were not realized, not least because of the complexity of the task, shortcomings in planning, and insufficient support from the authorities. In addition, the ideology of Official Nationality and the further advancement of Russian nationalism increasingly alienated large groups of former European subjects, particularly the Germans.

Sudden turn of destiny or forced resettlement?

The first time the Swedes on Dagö appeared in an official document was in 1470 when the Master of the Teutonic Order released them from the duty of daily labor in exchange for an annual fee of twenty Riga marks

---

⁴² Lohr, *Nationalizing the Russian Empire*, 4.
⁴³ Lohr, *Nationalizing the Russian Empire*, 84–120.
⁴⁴ *Nemtsy v istorii Rossii*, Diesendorf, 555–591.
⁴⁵ Lohr, *Nationalizing the Russian Empire*, 1.
⁴⁶ *Nemtsy v istorii Rossii*, Diesendorf, 558–562.

per district. These farmers were provided with a charter from the Master of the Order according to which they were allowed to live freely on the island, make a living as anglers, cultivate land and sell the products from their lands and forests. The Swedish settlements were mainly found in two districts on the northern part of the island. Swedes made up about a seventh of the total population of Dagö. The earliest duties of the Estonian Swedes were piloting ships, assisting in the salvaging of shipwrecks and providing the church with fish.

In 1561 when the rule of the Teutonic Order collapsed, the region was taken over by Sweden and new tax rules were introduced. The island remained under Swedish rule until 1710, when Russia invaded the Baltic region. The tax collectors of the Swedish Crown and their clerks made a list of all taxable farmers, Swedish as well as Estonian.

In the beginning, the tax collectors of the Swedish Crown respected the privileges of the Swedish farmers, granted by feudal law. Swedish monarchs issued new charters stipulating protection. The wars against Denmark, Poland and Muscovy, in which Sweden had been victorious, had for the most part been waged with borrowed means. The Swedish Crown was indebted to many military commanders. All that back pay was now to be cashed in and this was done mostly through selling conquered land or through awarding land to noblemen in Swedish service. In contrast to the Estonians, who had been enserfed after 1343, the Estonian Swedes had until that time managed to keep their personal freedom. In the years between 1590 and 1630, the free Swedish farmers living on Dagö came under the rule of feudal landlords who had no interest in respecting their privileges.

Count Jakob De la Gardie was given Dagö as an enfeoffment in 1620. King Gustavus II Adolphus then sold him the island in 1624 to keep in perpetuity as a fief. The situation of the Dagö-Swedes worsened even more when Axel-Julius De la Gardie inherited Dagö from his father. In 1659 the new landlord forbade the Dagö Swedes to trade freely with lime and cattle.

After many quarrels, Karl XI appointed a commission in Reval. The commission was to take a closer look at the complaints of the Swedish farmers in Estonia and ascertain their legal substance. The lawsuit ended with a compromise. Axel-Julius De la Gardie managed to divide the Swedish farmers into two groups. The Charters of the Grand Master of the German Order were deemed to be valid for the Swedes living in the villages of Röicks and Kertells. It is stated in a resolution from 7 October

1685 that the people living in the main villages were covered by the Charters but not the farmers in the neighboring villages. The remainder (approximately a third of the Dagö Swedes) was set on an equal footing with the Estonian serfs, unless they moved to Sweden.

In 1721 after the Nystad peace treaty, the Dagö Swedes requested that Peter I confirm their old privileges. Having received no reply, they repeated their request and the matter was given to the Restitution Commission that was founded by Catherine I. While waiting to hear from a descendant of Axel-Julius De la Gardie, the commission declined to make any decisions. By that time, Dagö belonged to the Russian Crown, which leased the island for shorter periods to officers and noblemen. The new possessors respected the exceptional position of the Swedes regarding their personal freedom, but demanded a workload and taxes equal to that of most Estonians.

In 1740, the Russian Senate made an important statement when the Estonian peasants were declared the personal property of their landlords. In 1755, the Russian Crown returned the estates on Dagö to the family of De La Gardie-Stenbock.

In the summer of 1779, the Swedish peasants on Dagö initiated legal action for their full freedom. On 17 January 1780, a temporary agreement was reached between Count Stenbock and his subjects. Stenbock recognized the freedom of the Swedes and the peasants were given the right to stay on their farms until March 1781, after which the matter would be re-examined – these were the key points of the agreement. Soon the situation was tense again between Count Stenbock and the Swedes. Consequently, Karl Magnus Stenbock sold his properties on Dagö to Baron Otto Reinhold Ludwig von Ungern-Sternberg.

The State Collegium of Justice in St Petersburg demanded that the new landowner should stick to the agreement of 17 January 1780 and give the peasants a six-month notice period. The peasants immediately sent a delegation to Baron Ungern-Sternberg and asked for permission to stay. On 9 March 1780 Baron Ungern-Sternberg agreed to grant this permission.

According to one version[47] Count Karl Magnus Stenbock, who knew Grigorii Potemkin personally, was the one who suggested that the

---

[47] For more about this development, see Jörgen Hedman, "När och varifrån kom den svenska befolkningen till Dagö?" in *Svenskbyborna 60 år i Sverige 1929–1989* (Visby: Bokförlaget Hanseproduktion, 1989) 20–34; Jörgen Hedman, Lars Åhlander, *Historien om Gammalsvenskby och svenskarna i Ukraina* (Stockholm: Dialogos, 2003); Jörgen

Swedish peasants could become a part of Russia's colonization policy. He, by chance, made an offer to Potemkin to resettle hard-working and capable Swedish peasants of Dagö Island in return for the liquidation of his debts. Stenbock intended to settle Estonian peasants in place of the Swedes who had brought him so much trouble. Potemkin, who was responsible for the colonization of the Azov and Black Sea territories, was having problems recruiting migrants and was very much interested in potential colonists. He encouraged Catherine II to proclaim a decree which would give the Dagö Swedes the chance to move to New Russia. A decree was issued on 8 March 1781, on the eve of the agreement between Baron Ungern-Sternberg and the Swedes.

Document 1: The Imperial Decree of Catherine II to the Estonia general-governor Board about the resettlement of the peasants of the manor of Körgessaare (Hohenholm) to New Russia province. 8 March 1781.

> Deigning the resettlement of the Swedish peasants of the manor of Hohenholm to New Russia province, who received the freedom from the former Master of the Teutonic Order and privileges and resolutions from the Swedish monarchs, confirmed by their present landowner Count Steinbock. He adds that the term of his engagement of the peasants lapsed after February of the present year. Thus, they must leave his lands. We are ruling to resettle these Swedish peasants, in total around 1000 persons female and male, to New Russia province in order accept them as state peasants*[48] of the local establishment.**[49] Therefore, the Reval *general-gubernatorskaia kantseliariia* is obliged to announce this will to all peasants, to compile their census and support them in the resettlement. Prince Potemkin, the governor-general of New Russia, Azov and Astrakhan, will be responsible for the fulfillment of the resettlement, for setting and allotting favorable state lands, for settling them and for their supplying.
>
> Catherine

Hedman, *Gammalsvenskby: the true story of the Swedish settlement in the Ukraine*, accessed October 20, 2010, http://www.svenskbyborna.com/Historia/Historiska%20dokument/Hedman%20Zmiivka%20history%20eng%20vers.htm.
*State peasants were considered free, but their movement was restricted. They were also bound to the land.
**The Kazykermen district of the New Russia province.

Source: Antifeodalnaia borba volnykh shvedskikh krestian Estliandii 18-19 vv., sbornik dokumentov, ed. Julius Madisson (Tallinn: Eesti raamat, 1978), 134-135.

A small group of Estonian Swedes was hardly central to the colonization of New Russia. However, having become accidentally involved with the colonization project in the recently expanded southern fringes of Russia, the Dagö Swedes were facing the possibility of ending their centuries-long judicial dispute with the landowners.

Such a solution to the conflict was also favorable for Potemkin. He was obliged to colonize the Azov and Black Sea territories and have them populated as soon as possible. Consequently, the decision satisfied Potemkin and Ungern-Sternberg, but it signified the beginning of a new ordeal for the Swedes. Potemkin persuaded Catherine II to issue a Decree on 8 March 1781 regarding the resettlement of approximately one thousand Swedish peasants from Hohenholm manor on the island of Dagö to the Kherson district near to the town of Kazikermen in the New Russia province.

Potemkin believed that the peasants would agree to move, if they were granted favorable conditions and some special privileges. He sent his representative, Colonel Ivan Sinelnikov, to Dagö, where he arrived on 10 July 1781. Sinelnikov gathered the Swedish peasants and explained the conditions for the settlement in the Black Sea territory. After some debate, the Swedes agreed to move. On 20 August 1781, a group of Swedes left their native island of Dagö forever.

Unlike German colonists, for instance, the Estonian Swedes were involved in the colonization of the recently acquired territory only by accident. Russia's government had never planned to set up large Swedish colonies in the Black Sea territory, as it had for Germans. Therefore, it is impossible to compare the place and role of Swedes and Germans in the mastering of the region. Potemkin's personal initiative to resettle the Swedes definitely influenced their destiny beyond this. Although actually being Russian subjects, the Swedes were granted the privileged status of colonists – just as foreign subjects from German states had been.[50]

---

[50] *Antifeodalnaia borba volnykh shvedskikh krestian Estliandii 18-19 vv., sbornik dokumentov*, ed. Julius Madisson (Tallinn: Eesti raamat, 1978), 31-34, 39-40, 52-53, 129-135, 141-142, 198-206, 325-326, 332-333, 350 pril.; Jörgen Hedman, "När och varifrån kom den svenska befolkningen till Dagö?" in *Svenskbyborna 60 år i Sverige 1929-1989* (Visby: Bokförlaget Hanseproduktion,1989) 20-34; Jörgen Hedman, Lars Åhlander, *Historien om Gammalsvenskby och svenskarna i Ukraina* (Stockholm: Dialogos, 2003); Hedman, *Gammalsvenskby: the true story*; Julia Malitska, *Estonski*

The migration of the Estonian Swedes from Dagö to the South seems to have been due to two main factors: the failed struggle to maintain their free judicial states and their old customs, and the concurrent promotion of large-scale colonization in the annexed Azov and Black Sea regions. While there was a general feeling of fatigue and hopelessness concerning the former, the latter opened a window of opportunity that a majority of the Swedish population of Dagö decided to take advantage of.

The contributions

By compiling the material from several archives and authors, Svitlana Bobyleva pursues the myth of the Gammalsvenskby Swedes' supposed bad treatment by the Russian state authorities. She argues that the trauma and massive loss of life during the migration and the initial years in southern Russia has cast a blurring shadow over the course of events. The Swedes were not forced to migrate, but accepted an offer that at the time seemed very generous given their distressed and unclear legal situation in Estonia. The inability of the authorities to support the Swedes, during the initial years of the settlement in southern Russia, was due to the lack of knowledge of the territory where the settlement was taking place and the fragmentary character of the regional administration. Once efficient administrators who were aware of the local conditions began to act, conditions for the Swedes improved greatly; they were even officially granted the colonist status they had so far enjoyed de facto. Bobyleva also punctuates the myth about the broken promises concerning the acreage of land provided to the Swedes, showing that the land was redistributed in 1804 due to the significantly reduced number of Swedish families as compared to 1781. The 34 families that had survived required much less land than the 200 families that originally left Dagö, according to the authorities' calculations. The redistribution also took place at a time when the abundance of land available in the late eighteenth century had turned into a growing scarcity of land for distribution among the colonists who were arriving in droves.

---

shvedy na Pivdni Rosiiskoi imperii: mihratsiia, adaptatsiia ta aculturatsiia pereselentsiv-colonistiv (1781–1871) [The Estonian Swedes in the South of the Russian Empire: Migration, Adaptation and Acculturation of the Migrants-Colonists (1781–1871)]. Manuscript of the Candidate thesis (Dnipropetrovsk, 2010), 61–77.

Julia Malitska's chapter illuminates the process of acculturation of the villagers of Gammalsvenskby from the migration from Dagö to the withdrawal of their colonist status in 1871. The term "acculturation" allows the studying of the processes of adaptation to the new milieu as in-making and partial, rather than as a straightforward way towards assimilation. Malitska finds that after the initial shocks caused by the hardships of the migration, and different climatic and geographical conditions of the new settlement that resulted in drastic initial demographic losses, the village began to successfully integrate into the ever changeable milieu of the southern fringes of the Russian Empire. New methods of agricultural production were adopted and new complementary sources of income were found. The Swedes did this in interaction with the authorities, and their Russian, Ukrainian and German neighbors, but without giving up the basic features of their native culture. It may be argued that their knowledge of German and Russian made it easier for them to keep their old customs and hold on to their traditional religion. The mastering of both languages gave fruitful neighborly interaction, good commercial relationships and allowed good contacts with the colonist authorities, something that the Swedes' German neighbors frequently lacked. Due to their ability to communicate with basically everyone, the villagers of Gammalsvenskby were more or less free to safeguard their customs. Nevertheless, not merely the material, but the spiritual culture of the villagers was slowly changing, becoming vulnerable to stronger assimilation currents in the decades after 1871.

Piotr Wawrzeniuk studies the creation of the village as it was understood in Sweden and Finland during the three decades preceding the First World War. The author suggests that the villagers preserved their Swedish identity due to their relative isolation from the surrounding society and to the fact that they could therefore retain characteristics which are usually considered typical of peasants in the early modern period. The visit by Finnish-Swedophone linguist Herman Vendell to the village marked the start of a period when Gammalsvenskby was integrated into an all-Swedish context, where nationalistic and romantic views of common ancestry as a tool of identification and unification were dominant. Although several visitors to the village noticed that the villagers had been affected by a century of living in southern Russia, a way of reasoning prevailed where the population was automatically included in the Swedish nation. The visitors to the village from Sweden and Finland mirrored the advent of modernity in these countries. The cultural differentiation within both countries proved influential for the future development of Gammalsvenskby. The author brings forward the examples of Herman Vendell and the Swedish missionary Emma Skarstedt. They were influenced by the very specific cultural and political contexts of Finland and Sweden respectively. Their beliefs, shaped in the home countries, functioned as a prism through which the situation in the village was seen. The romantic and nationalistic view presented by Vendell would dominate the image of the village prior to the migration of most of the villagers to Sweden in 1929. Following that, it became obvious that the Gammalsvenskby inhabitants were influenced as much by their Swedish roots as by living for 147 years in the specific milieu of southern Russia.

Andrej Kotljarchuk's chapter explores virtually unknown aspects of the development during the 1930s. The author shows how a disillusioned group of 265 former Gammalsvenskby villagers who returned to the USSR in 1930–31 became a piece in a propaganda game orchestrated from the USSR. After the split within the Swedish Communist Party (SKP), the branch loyal to the Comintern took the opportunity to flex its muscles politically in Sweden on the one hand, and prove it to be an efficient part of the Comintern, on the other. The Comintern considered that SKP had neglected the rural question; now the time was ripe to correct this mistake in great style by bringing about the re-migration of the dissenting group of villagers. Kotljarchuk uses the concept of techniques of forced normalization, and proceeds with a closer study of the configuration of new boundaries, one of the aspects of forced normalization. He unveils the creation of a new vision of history and future. This included a new image of the oppressed and the oppressors, the introduction of a collective farm (*kolkhoz*) as a way of proceeding towards the bright Communist future, new administrative boundaries and new linguistic practices (the name Gammalsvenskby was changed to "Röda Svenskby," Red Swedish Village), along with a number of other novelties. A new hierarchy was also created for Swedish and Finno-Swedish Communists, and new cadres were drilled in the local *Komsomol*, replacing the (absent) traditional elite of successful farmers and the moral authority of the (absent) local priest. However, the project was abruptly ended by the *Holodomor*, the man-made famine that raged across Soviet Ukraine 1932–33 reaching Röda Svenskby in the fall of 1932. Faced with new problems and abandoned by the Swedish

Communists, the farmers petitioned the authorities just as their forefathers sent supplications to lords and royalties. There were also calls for Sweden to help. The author finds these acts to be ones of fading collective resistance that ceased due to the Stalinist terror in 1937–38, when twenty-three villagers were taken away and secretly executed.

Nowopetrowskoje
Fl. Bug
Fedorowka
Pereszadowka
Matwijewka
Ternowka
Woskreszenskoje
Nikolajew
Nikolajewka
Jantschakrak
Bugskoje Liman
Kiszliakowka
Chutor
Alexandrowka
Sztanislaw
Sawilowo
Traktir
Szadowoje
Nikolskoje
CHERSON
Iwanowskoje
Aleschki
Kardaschyni
Belaja Prisztan
Sburrewszk
Michailowka
Dnieper See
LIMAN
Ur. Burkuly
Ur. Szaryki Kopp.
Burghun
Rendra oder Tenter
Koska Tenter
Koska Dschharilghatsch

Previous pages: **Map 4:** Probably the first appearance of Gammalsvenskby ("Schwedszkaja Kolonija") on a map. Kezikermen, the nearest hamlet, was renamed Berislav ("Beriszlaw") circa 1789–1805, Krigsarkivet 0403/31/A/037 18a.

Map 5: Swedes and their neighbours. "Old Swedish" [colony] is now accompanied by the villages of Mühlhausendorf and Klosterdorf to the south, and along the road Berislav. *Special map of the western part of the Russian Empire* ("Spets. Karta Zap. Chasti Rossiiskoi Imperii G.L. Schuberta"), 1826–1840, Krigsarkivet, 0403/31/32/LI

The Russian State and Swedes in New Russia (between the eighteenth and nineteenth centuries)

SVITLANA BOBYLEVA

In the literature on Gammalsvenskby it is often said that the Dagö Swedes were forced to move to the South of the Russian Empire. This belief has old roots, and is based on the inscription on the cross erected near the church of Gammalsvenskby in the nineteenth century. In contemporary Ukraine, this historiography has unfortunately been turned into mythologization. This chapter will identify the most common myths and then, in their place, give an account of the course of events based on documents.

In 1995 professor Hanna Chumachenko called upon scholars to look into the reasons and character of the interaction of different cultures in Zmiivka. Using old residents' accounts and a few historical documents Chumachenko confidently stated that Catherine II expelled the Swedes from the Baltic island of Dagö in 1782.[1] This statement might have passed unnoticed, particularly as the Chumachenko is a philologist, and not a professional historian, but Chumachenko returned to the subject in 1997, claiming that force was used against the Estonian Swedes when they were deported. In addition, she suggested that by accusing the whole ethnic group of plundering, Catherine II stirred feelings of collective guilt among the Swedish settlers.[2]

The term "deportation" appears three times on two pages in Chumachenko's article. She also defined the settlement of Swedish prisoners-of-war in Gammalsvenskby in 1790 as deportation. Moreover,

---

[1] Hanna Chumachenko, "Kulturnyi prostir pivdnia," *Naddniprianska Ukraina*, January 31, 1995.
[2] Hanna Chumachenko, "Shvedske poselennia na Pivdni Ukrainy," *Narodna tvorchist ta etnografiia*, no. 2–3 (1997), 105.

she claimed the Swedes took the risky decision to resettle because there was an imminent threat of enserfment; and that Catherine II granted the Swedes colonist status only during a visit to the region, when she was accompanied by foreigners and wished to conceal the very difficult situation of the Swedes.[3] Among related interpretations of the nature of the Swedes' movement to the South of the Russian Empire one finds Anatolii Kusheverski, who described it as "free-will deportation,"[4] and Alexander Loit who characterized it as 'administrative removal."[5]

Document 2: About the Swedish colony in the remote places of Russia.

/.../ Swedes who under unheard repression had long lived a miserable life on Dagö, where they uncountable times begged the Russian government for permission to move away /.../

Source: "En svensk koloni i djupa Ryssland," *Helsingfors Aftonblad*, 1893.06.20, no.25.

Myths and reality

The turns of fortune of the "Swedes" before the eighteenth century are well known. They used to help ship-wreck survivors, provide clergymen and parishioners with fish, and they were personally free. But then things happened which explain why they left Dagö.

When Count Jakob De la Gardie in 1624 attempted to enserf the Swedish peasants, he encountered firm resistance. The Swedes defended their personal freedom on the whole successfully but the year 1721 marked a turning point. The territory and its population passed to Russia, and the threats to the personal freedom of the Swedes increased. In their struggle, they chose the method of requesting and petitioning, a defense very different to the spontaneous riots of the Russians, or the violent

---

[3] Hanna Chumachenko, "Fenomen "kulturnogo shoku" na Pivdni Ukrainy ta iogo literaturni retsenzii," in *Zaselennia Pivdnia Ukrainy: problemy natsionalnogo ta kulturnoho rozvytku:naukovi rozpovidi Mizhnarodnoi naukovo-metodychnoi konferentsii (21–24 travnia 1997)*, ch. 2 (Kherson, 1997), 211–215; "Shvedy pod Khersonom. Pod Poltavoi shvedy byli bity. A pod Khersonom – prizhylis," *Khersonskyi visnyk*, no.4/21(1993), 5.
[4] Anatolii Kusheverskii, "K voprosu o perspektivakh issledovaniia shvedskikh obshchin v Rossii v 19 veke v fondakh RGIA," in *Materialy konferentsii "Sankt-Peterburg i strany Severnoi Evropy,"* accessed February 10, 2009, http://www.rchgi.spb.ru/spb/conference_1/kusheversky.htm.
[5] Alexander Loit, "Pereselenie shvedov iz Estonii na Ukrainu v kontse 18 veka," in *Skandinavskii zbornik*, no.32 (Tallinn: Eesti paamat, 1988), 105.

protests of the free Zaporizhian Cossacks. From the 1770s, their opponent in this legal struggle was Count Stenbock, the husband of Count De la Gardie's granddaughter. They hired a lawyer and organized a delegation to the Court of Justice of Reval province.

The chronology of the events that occurred is as follows: on 18 July 1779, Count Stenbock replied to the Court that he gave the Swedes back their freedom and on 5 September 1779, he demanded that within a six-month term they should leave his land. In December 1779, the Court in Reval confirmed the lawfulness of these actions. The Swedes responded by taking their case to the State Collegium of Justice in St Petersburg. Weary of lawsuits and not sure that the verdict of St Petersburg lawyers would be in his favor, Stenbock sold his property on Dagö to Baron Otto Reinhold Ludwig von Ungern-Sternberg.[6]

Meanwhile other events were taking place in Russia. Following its victory over Turkey in the 1768–1774 war, Russia started developing the Black Sea territory and populating the so-called Wild Field. In view of the existing conflict, the Swedes were given the opportunity (the Imperial Decree of 8 March 1781) to settle in New Russia on quite favorable terms.

Almost simultaneously, 9 March 1781, Ungern-Sternberg permitted the Swedes, those who had been most active in resisting him, to stay on his island. Thus, the Swedes were facing the dilemma of whether to stay on the baron's land (*not* their own land), which several of them would be forced to leave anyway, or move to the new lands with the promise of good prospects.

If one compares what would be left of the Swedish ownership of land, and what they were promised, migration seems to be the rational step. On Dagö, the average farmer had 13.8 *desiatinas*[7] of arable land, one horse, two oxen, and one cow. The Swedes were promised sixty *desiatinas* of arable land per household for use in perpetuity, combined with various financial and tax privileges. This must surely be the explanation for why the Swedes chose to move. Alexander Loit estimates that the fate of the Swedes was impossible to avert once Catherine II's order had been issued.[8] However, we know that 75 Swedish peasants refused to resettle and moved to Reval. Moreover, if the

---

[6] Marquis de Kustin wrote about Karl Ungern-Sternberg.
[7] *Desiatina* (Russian: десятина) Old Russian unit of land area. The desiatina originally measured 1,092 hectares.
[8] Loit, "Pereselenie shvedov," 105.

peasants were simply forced to obey the order, and act against their own will, there would have been no reason for Colonel Ivan Sinelnikov's propagandist mission. Yet it started on 10 July 1781, and its results are well known.

In historical literature, there are several estimates as to the number of the Swedes who left Dagö. The exact number of those who left in 1781 is important to determine; the higher the original number of migrants, the higher the human losses suffered during the initial period, and vice versa. The number on the list created by the officials of Reval Governorate Chancellery was 935 individuals.[9] However, by that time 75 people who did not wish to resettle, notwithstanding the promises made to them, had already left the island. Yet the number of resettlers on the list before the departure was 960 persons. Andrej Kotljarchuk writes about 1,000 resettlers,[10] while Alexander Loit gives the figure 1,200.[11] One of the Kherson editions mentioned 880 Swedes from Dagö.[12] The figure given in the Senate report from the year 1800 is 904 persons. Jörgen Hedman writes about 1,207 people who wished to resettle. The resettlers and the vicar from the neighboring island provided the same numbers.[13] However, one should remember that the accounts of ordinary people – the first resettlers – constitute part of their reaction to the extraordinary and traumatic events. The accounts have then been passed on from one generation to the next, becoming a virtual canon of local memory.

As various official documents differ on the matter, I suggest making use of the financial document – the rough-copy list of the departing Swedes, available at the Dnipropetrovsk Oblast archive. It was drawn up on 26 August 1781. The character of the material suggests it is authentic. The list contains the number of the departing Swedes, of their belongings, and of the travel expenses granted to them for the two-and-a-half

---

[9] Julia Malitska, "Shvedske naselennia Pivdnia Rosiiskoi imperii: peredumovy, prychyny na khid migratsii," in *Visnyk Chernihivskoho derzhavnoho pedahohichnogo universytetu*, vyp. 52, seriia: Istorychni nauky, no.5 (Chernihiv: Chernihivskyi Derzhavnyi pedahohichnyi universytet, 2008), 23.
[10] Andrej Kotjarchuk, "Nemtsy Ukrainy v sudbakh shvedskoi kolonii na Dnepre, 1805–2007" in *Voprosy germanskoi istorii*, ed. Svetlana Bobyleva (Dnipropetrovsk: Porogi, 2007), 28.
[11] Loit, "Pereselenie shvedov," 106.
[12] *Zabuttiu ne pidliahae. Narysy. Spogady. Opovidannia*, ed. Eduard Dubovyk (Kherson: "Reabilitovani istorieiu," 1994), 224.
[13] Jörgen Hedman, *Gammalsvenskby - the true story of the Swedish settlement in the Ukraine*, accessed 22 April 2010, http://www.svenskbyborna.com/Historia/Historiska%20dokument/Hedman%20Zmiivka%20history%20eng%20vers.htm

month journey. The document also provides a full picture of the sex-and-age structure of the resettlers.[14]

The Dnipropetrovsk list numbers 482 men and 485 women, giving a total of 967 individuals. Nevertheless, the nominal list – with all the names given – runs to 965 persons. Proceeding from the above-mentioned, we can say that the number of Swedes who left for New Russia was 965.

As to the date the colony was founded, there also exists a certain discrepancy: the Senate report from the year 1800 mentions 1787.[15] This date appears also in the work by Alexander Klaus[16] and in the materials of the journal *Severnyi archiv*.[17] Andrej Kotljarchuk[18] and Vasilii Kabuzan[19] refer to 1781 as the foundation date. Ivan Kulinich,[20] Hanna Chumachenko,[21] Alexander Loit[22] and Jörgen Hedman[23] write about 1782. We know that the Swedes left Dagö on 20 August 1781. On 26 November 1781, they reached the village of Reshetilovka located 25 kilometers from Poltava. The village was assigned to be their winter quarters. On 16 April 1782, the group was to pick up the journey to the place of settlement, as the time was ripe to start spring-field works.[24] In other words, the Swedes settled on the territory of the colony in the spring of 1782. As to the year 1781, in the context of the foundation of Gammalsvenskby, it might be related to the dating of Catherine II's Decree regarding the resettlement of the Swedes, and not to the date that the colony was founded.

Another misconception in the history of Gammalsvenskby is the supposedly broken promise from the side of the Russian state. No houses had been built for the Swedes and no fields had been sown before their arrival. Below, I intend to clarify what happened and look for a possible explanation. The resettlement terms delimit the obligations of

---

[14] DAOO, f.134, op. 1, spr. 1, arkk. 2–3.
[15] PSZRI, sobr. 1, t. 26, str. 119.
[16] Alexander Klaus, *Nashi kolonii. Opyt i materialy po istorii i statistike inostrannoi kolonizatsii v Rossii*, vyp.1(Sankt-Peterburg: Tip. V.V. Nusvalta, 1869), 568.
[17] *Severnyi archive: Zhurnal istorii, statistiki i puteshestvii*, no.8, April, 1824, 64.
[18] Kotjarchuk, "Nemtsy Ukrainy v sudbakh shvedskoi kolonii na Dnepre," 28.
[19] Vasilii Kabuzan, *Zaselenie Novorossii v 18 i pervoi polovine 19 vv.* (Moskva: Nauka, 1976), 176.
[20] Ivan Kulinich, "Iak i koly ziavylysia shvedski kolonii v Pivdennii Ukraini," *Ukrainskyi istorychnyi zhurnal*, no.1 (1995), 120.
[21] Chumachenko, "Shvedske poselennia na Pivdni Ukrainy," 102.
[22] Loit, "Pereselenie shvedov," 106.
[23] Hedman, *Gammalsvenskby - the true story*.
[24] Grirorii Pisarevskii, "Pereselenie shvedov s ostrova Dago v Novorossiiskii krai (Po dokumentam Gosudarstvennogo arkhiva)," *Russkii vestnik*, kn. 3 (Moskva, 1899), 250.

the state. According to the terms, the resettlers would be given a sufficient lot of fertile land in the New Russia province, sixty *desiatinas* per household. During the four initial years they would be granted preferential duties, but with further commitment to pay the State Treasury the same amount as other state settlers – five *dengas*[25] per *desiatina* for a year – after the initial period expired. On the other hand, they would no longer pay the poll tax. The settlers would be given a writ and a payment of twelve rubles per household for building and setting up a house. They would be provided with seeds for sowing and food supplies for a year. In new places they would be settled in "special colonies", i.e. separate from settlers of other nationalities, and would have their own church and priest. On their way to the places of settlement they would be rendered all possible assistance.[26] Thus, there is no mention of either houses to be erected or fields sown before the settlers' arrival. However, while the Swedes were on their way to new places Grigorii Potemkin ordered the governor of the New Russia province Nikolai Iazykov to apportion sixty *desiatinas* of land along the bank of the Dnipro up to the town of Kazykermen to the Swedish settlers. A portion of the woodlands on the nearby islands would be reserved for the Swedes' common use. The governor was also instructed to buy seeds for sowing at the province's expense, to gather oxen and ploughs from Zaporizhian *zymnyks*,[27] and to plough and sow twelve *chetveriks*[28] of grain per household by the fall of 1781. As the Swedes had planned to reach their colony in the late fall, the governor should "choose well-disposed settling areas and place the Swedes there for the winter period providing them with free food supplies."

In addition, Potemkin gave orders to Iazykov that the houses should be built under the supervision of carpenters brought from Kurland, so that the type of building would be familiar to the resettlers.[29] This part of Potemkin's order[30] illustrates that he was not well informed about the physical character of the resettlement area. The document mentions

---

[25] *Denga* (Russian: деньга) was a Russian monetary unit with a value latterly equal to ½ kopeck (100 kopecks = 1 Russian Ruble).
[26] Pisarevskii, "Pereselenie shvedov," 247.
[27] *Zymnyk* (Ukrainian: зимник) was a name for the Zaporizhian Cossaks' winter camps, sixteenth to eighteenth centuries.
[28] *Chetverik* (Russian: четверик) Old Russian unit of volume, 1 chetverik was equal to 26, 24 liters. The word "chetverik" means "one fourth" or "one quarter."
[29] Pisarevskii, "Pereselenie shvedov," 250.
[30] "Order" – this was the name of the document.

"woodland places on the islands," but there was no timber there, there was only "firewood."[31] There was a shortage of timber in the Azov and Black Sea territories.[32]

The people who undertook the work of planning, populating the area and developing it economically, were, as it turned out, unaware of the real conditions in the locality to which they sent the first settlers. In the case of the Swedes, they were really the first to settle in the area. The administration responsible for their accommodation simply had no experience, but developed methods of organizing the settlers' everyday life. This situation was typical of the system of power from the top to the bottom. Proof of this can be found even in Catherine II's manifesto of 1763, in the part that concerns lands. They are described as free and suitable for populating, in particular so the Barabin Steppe with its forests, rivers, fisheries and fertile land.[33] However, the Barabin Steppe bears its name exactly because it is a steppe. Consequently, there are no forests there – only small groups of birch trees, vast swamps, feather-grass steppes, snowdrifts and frosts.

The documents of the eighteenth and nineteenth centuries concerning the region frequently mention its lack of timber. This problem urged Samuel Contenius, the head of the colonist administration, to pay special attention to forest planting. However, at the same time he understood that the colonists could not start until 1815, as production of the "daily bread" on a sufficient scale had to be achieved first.[34]

The shortage of timber, its high cost, problems of delivering it to its destination, and the repeated efforts of the colonist administration to solve the timber problem – constitute the subject of numerous documents and are worthy of a special investigation.[35] But all of them belong to the beginning of the nineteenth century whereas the events concerning "our" Swedes are dated from the early 1780s. The scarcity of timber in the area where the Swedish village was founded and an overall shortage in the region made the materialization of Potemkin's aspirations to build houses for the colonists unrealistic. Of course, people tried to find alternatives. The governor Iazykov thought that natural stone,

---

[31] *Severnyi archiv*, s. 66.
[32] Pisarevskii, "Pereselenie shvedov," 250.
[33] PSZRI, sobr. 1, t. 26, str. 315–316.
[34] DAOO, f. 6, op. 1, spr. 969, ark. 108.
[35] RGIA, f. 383, op. 29, l. 3-b; DADO, f. 134, op. 1, spr. 54, arkk. 57–58; DADO, f. 134, op.1, spr.72, ark.133; DAOO, f. 6, op. 1, spr.138, arkk. 216, 653–671.

which was available "near the area allotted to resettlers," would provide a durable and cheap building material for colonist houses. Yet originally, the first Swedish settlers had to erect earth-shelters and live in them until regular houses were built.[36] Apparently, those earth-shelters proved to be strong and durable; in 1804 they functioned as temporary shelter for German colonists who were settled as neighbors of the Swedes.[37]

The situation with winter sowing was also far from safe. If it was possible to plough the virgin Wild Field and sow seeds, as Potemkin's order implied, there would have been no need to call upon the colonists. In this particular case (with no fields sown beforehand), what really mattered was the "human factor" and the shortage of agricultural tools.[38] In other words, it was the result of incompetent Russian governance, caused by a lack of knowledge of the local conditions and/or fragmentary administration.

The land issue

1804 marks a turning point in the life of the Swedish colony. During that year, German colonists were settled on its land. The settlement reduced the acreage of available land. The withdrawal of land from the population of Gammalsvenskby has generally been interpreted as yet another aggravation against the Swedish orchestrated by the Russian state. I shall argue that this action was a part of general state policy, and followed the regulations as to how the land was to be distributed.

Initially it was believed that 200 families of Estonian Swedes would migrate to New Russia. Every family would be allotted sixty *desiatinas* of land. Hence, the total of the land allotted to the Swedish settlers made 12,000 *desiatinas*. However, only 127 families left Dagö. Correspondingly, the land required should then be 7,620 *desiatinas*. Thus, the acreage allotted to each Swedish family considerably exceeded the area that was originally intended.

That would not have been entirely unreasonable if the population of the village had grown fast in the ensuing years, or if there had at least been a prospect of fast growth. However, the demographic situation in the

---

[36] Pisarevskii, "Pereselenie shvedov," 250.
[37] *Severnyi arkhiv*, 67. In 1924, "Severnyi arkhiv" (The Northern Archive) wrote that the Swedish houses were wooden, but the Germans had dugout houses covered with straw.
[38] In 1811, the density of local population was 5.4 persons per *versta* (1 versta=1,068 kilometers).

course of migration and at the initial stage of settlement and adaptation was depressing. Several factors led to just over half of the Swedes reaching their destination. The choice of season for the movement was erroneous – it was fall with rains, early frosts and winds, affecting the Swedes' health adversely. The route was long and hard. Another important factor was the age composition of the settlers; 36 per cent of the settlers who set off to the south were children under the age of sixteen. Out of these children, 13 per cent were aged between six months to five years; eight babies at the time of movement were not even six months.[39] The children suffered more than others as they were more vulnerable to the cold and infectious diseases. Along the way, in Belarus, the Swedes became infected with small-pox, resulting in several deaths. When they stopped for the winter in Poltava province, they numbered no more than 880 individuals, down from 965.

In January 1782, Iazykov reported that thirty adults and fifty-six children had died. Living conditions after the settlement appear to have been even harder. Between July 1782 and March 1783, 336 people died. By the spring of 1783, only 148 Swedes were alive. The causes were mainly the terrible conditions on the way, infectious diseases typical of that time, and a lack of medical assistance. In addition, the dwellings in which the Swedes had made their homes were unfit for permanent habitation (earth-shelters that were both damp and cold). As they were not accustomed to the climatic conditions, they fell prey to malaria and typhus. There was a lack of fresh water. The settlers were "to be in the habit of enduring those hardships, so that right at the beginning not to lose their energy and feel sorrow for the native land they had left," wrote Dmitrii Bagalei.[40] The situation in the colony made the government look for an immediate solution. In 1790 another thirty-one Swedes – former prisoners-of-war, who wished to become Russian citizens – were settled there. However, living conditions in the colony obviously did not suit the newcomers; the large majority of them left and only between five[41] and nine individuals remained.[42]

On 8 November 1796 Catherine II died. The Catherinean age was marked by an active colonization policy. The new Emperor, Paul I, was

---

[39] Malitska, "Shvedske naselennia Pivdnia Rosiiskoi imperii," 24.
[40] Dmitrii Bagalei, *Kolonizatsiia Novorossiiskogo kraia i pervye shagi ego po puti kultury* (Kiev: Tip. G. T. Korchak-Novitskogo, 1889), 100.
[41] Kotjarchuk, "Nemtsy Ukrainy v sudbakh shvedskoi kolonii na Dnepre," 29.
[42] Bagalei, *Kolonizatsiia Novorossiiskogo kraia*, 91.

difficult to understand as a political figure. After inheriting the throne, he changed political course entirely from that of his mother.[43] Still, as far as colonization was concerned it seems as if he wished to continue his mother's policy. Moreover, his energetic measures to improve the situation in the colonies could have helped to reinvigorate the colonists. However, in 1801 he was assassinated. His successor Alexander I chose to follow the Catherinean settlement policy, but also to make use of the results of Paul I's policy. He took further steps to colonize the Azov and Black Sea territories. At that time settlement practice was dominated by the German population, as Alexander I was strongly influenced by the pro-German circles in the Court. The years 1803–1811 constituted the peak of German colonization; in the Kherson province alone, 33 German agricultural colonies were founded.[44]

The great influx of colonists meant that more land was needed for distribution. Unexpectedly, a shortage of available land became apparent. After Zaporizhian Sich had been ruined in 1775, the Russian authorities started a redistribution process of its lands to private persons, officials, military officers, landowners, and foreigners. They also received land in newly conquered territories. Only smallholders, peasants and landowners' serfs were excluded from the land distribution.[45] The size of land lots varied from 1,500 to 12,000 *desiatinas*, but some people obtained up to tens of thousands of *desiatinas*. The terms were quite generous: populating the lot and putting the land into agricultural use. The people who obtained the land were exempt from all taxes and duties for a period of ten years. If the terms were observed, the land could then be turned into the user's private property. However, at the turn of the nineteenth century it became clear that the process of economic development of the southern territories was slowing down. The land distribution did not generate the effect the authorities had expected. By 1792, the new territories still remained sparsely populated, and the government decided to grant landholders another four years to populate their lots. Those who did not fill the quota fixed in their contract had to return the extra land to the State Treasury. In compen-

---

[43] Fedor Golovkin, *Dvor i tsarstvovanie Pavla I* (Moskva, 1912); Nikolai Shylder, *Imperator Alexander I: ego zhizn i tsarstvovanie*, t. 1–2 (Sankt-Peterburg: Izdanie A.S. Suvorina, 1904); Alexander Vallotton, *Alexander I* (Moskva: Progress, 1991).
[44] *Ocherki istorii nemtsev i mennonitov Iuga Ukrainy (konets 18–19 pervaia polovina 19 vekov)*, ed. Svetlana Bobyleva (Dnipropetrovsk: Art-press, 1999), 42.
[45] Bagalei, *Kolonizatsiia Novorossiiskogo kraia*, 70.

sation they were paid eighty *kopecks* per *desiatina*. The withdrawn land could be then allotted to colonists or sold to private individuals at the same price, eighty *kopecks* per *desiatina*.[46] The Swedish colony was also affected by this process.

Starting in 1803, the authorities actively searched for new land for settlement. Decisions were taken to withdraw land from officers and generals[47] who did not adhere to the terms of obtaining the land.[48] Part of the lands owned by landlords was sequestered by the State Treasury in order to be used by colonists.[49] Lands were bought from state officials[50] and were repossessed from landlords for non-payment of land tax.[51] Lots of land was cut off from state settlements.[52] Land-surveyors inspected the region, searching for vacant land.[53]

Amidst this search, the Guardianship Office for Foreign Settlers could not leave unnoticed the lands of the Swedish colony, where 34 families were in possession of land originally allotted to 200 families (12,000 *desiatinas*). The land belonging to the Swedes should only have totalled 2,040 *desiatinas*.[54] For a variety of reasons, they did not even use that acreage to the full. Cultivating crops did not suffice for their needs at the time (due to drought, a shortage of agricultural implements and the presence of vermin). Fishing was their major occupation. The 1802 report from the caretaker (*smotritel*) of the Swedish colony Ivan Pavlowski to *Kontora opekunstva* stated: "The Swedish colonists do not work hard to sow spring crops and show no diligence to till the soil."[55] Taking into account this situation, it was decided on 9 July 1804 to settle German colonists on the surplus lands of the Swedish colony. Afterwards those German settlers founded three colonies – Klosterdorf, Mühlhausendorf and Schlangendorf.[56]

---

[46] Bagalei, *Kolonizatsiia Novorossiiskogo kraia*, 75.
[47] *Zapiski Odesskogo obschestva istorii i drevnostei*, t. 24 (Odessa: Ekonomichaskaia tipografiia i litografiia, 1902) 36–37.
[48] DADO, f. 134, op. 1, d.72, ll. 9–10.
[49] RGIA, f. 383, op. 29, d. 217, ll. 18–22; *Pisma gertsoga Amana Emmanuel De Richelieu Samueliu Khristianovichu Conteniusu. 1803–1814*, ed. Olga Konovalova (Odessa: OKFA "TES," 1999), 212–213.
[50] RGIA, f. 383, op. 29, d. 217, ll. 18–22.
[51] DADO, f. 134, op. 1, d. 72, ll. 16–17.
[52] DAOO, f. 1, op. 220, d.13, ll. 250.
[53] RGIA, f. 383, op. 29, d. 205, l. 54; DADO, f. 134, op. 1, d. 72, l. 15.
[54] DAOO, f. 1, op. 220, spr. 4, ark. 124.
[55] DAOO, f. 6, op. 1, spr. 98, arkk. 71–72.
[56] DADO, f. 134, op. 1, spr. 72, ark. 51.

In other words, the withdrawal of land from the Swedish colonists was not an act of ill-will, nor a violation of their rights, or a breaking of earlier obligations by the state administration. It was the result of the prevailing state of things in the colony, as well as of the state policy at that time towards all agriculturalists in the region.

Table 1: The number of families in the Swedish colonist district (1800–1887).

	1800	1804	1812 – 1815	1821	1836	1859	1887
Gammalsvenskby	22	34	30	40	40	40	71
Klosterdorf	-	-	30	33	33	35	70
Mühlhausendorf	-	-	16	18	21	35	57
Schlangendorf	-	-	19	28	32	35	50

Source: Materialy dlia otsenki zemel Khersonskoi gubernii, t. 6. Khersonskii uezd (statistiko-ekonomicheskoe opisanie uezda), (Kherson: Tip. O.D. Khodushynoi, 1890), 147–148; DAKhO, f. 14, op. 1, d. 36, l. 44, 58; DAOO, f. 6, op.1, d. 4458, l. 117.

Table 1 shows that although the number of families diminished in some years, there was a tendency towards an increase in the second half of the nineteenth century. Thus, the number of families grew while the acreage available to the villagers remained the same. This process brought about the "land problem" and the judicial wrestling that began in the late nineteenth century.

A question that remains to be answered is why the Swedes were given sixty *desiatinas* of land. Resettlers with Russian citizenship – *starovery, raskolniki, dukhobory*,[57] the state peasants – were given no more than fifteen *desiatinas* per household. On what basis did the Swedish settlers claim privileges for 30 years? All colonists were only granted ten years. Since 1800 at the latest there are no traces of the document according to which the Swedes were settled in the Kherson region.

---

[57] Eighteenth century religious denominations that opposed the official Russian Orthodox Church were persecuted for disobedience to the authorities and refusal to serve in the army; they migrated to Canada at the end of the nineteenth century.

Military service

When in 1874 compulsory military service was introduced in Russia, the Swedes objected that the new law should not apply to them. However, the reform encompassed all estates and was motivated by the political situation outside Russia and the necessity to strengthen the country's defenses. The army needed new principles of recruitment. Minister of Defense Dmitrii Miliutin wrote:

> It was meant to annul a great number of outdated articles of the previous recruitment regulations /.../ to lay the burden of military service upon as large a number of people as possible and in this way make easier the lot of that part of population which had been bearing that burden before. It was a delicate task. With our estate privileges and various favors given at different times to some or other categories of population, what criterion should be accepted in the new legislative work?[58]

The inhabitants of Dagö had since 1721 been Russian subjects, and it was quite natural that the Swedes were, like all other colonists who were Russian subjects, to be the part of conscription. The terms on which the Swedes were invited to settle in the south did not include exemption from military service. Yet there was a catch. From the time they moved to Ukraine, the Swedes were de facto treated as colonists. In 1800 they were granted the status of foreign colonists, and the document had a clause detailing colonists' exemption from the military service.[59]

Beginning in 1874 all colonists including the Swedes were obliged to serve in the armed forces. Times and circumstances were changing and not only in Russia. In Europe as well as in the USA a program of integrating the population into the consolidated whole – civic society – was underway. It was accompanied by the unification of legislation and forms of governing the territories. In this process, uniform rights and duties of citizens were introduced.

A question that remains to be answered is why the Swedes were given sixty *desiatinas* of land. Resettlers with Russian citizenship – *starovery*,

---

[58] *Otdel rukopisei Gosudarstvennoi Rossiiskoi biblioteki, fond Dmitriia Miliutina*, M. 7850, str. 91–92.
[59] PSZRI, sobr. 1, t. 26, no. 19372, str. 115–128.

raskolniki, dukhobory,⁶⁰ the state peasants – were given no more than fifteen *desiatinas* per household. What privileged thirty-year period did the Swedes claim in 1800? All the colonists were granted ten privileged years. Since 1800 at the latest there are no traces of the document according to which the Swedes were settled in the Kherson region.

Authorities and colonists

Russia has been called the jail of peoples, and there is no doubt that Tsarist Russia was unjustifiably cruel to indigenous peoples in the eighteenth and nineteenth centuries. However, the position of foreign colonists could not be compared with that of Russian serfs.

When discussing the problem of the Russian state's attitude towards the Swedes, we cannot separate it from the problem of foreign colonization in general, i.e. the attitude of the state power towards Germans, Mennonites, French and other settlers in New Russia. From the very start of the colonization, the Russian rulers of the eighteenth century through to the beginning of the nineteenth century considered the populating of New Russia a top priority. They took personal interest in the economic development of the colonies and directed the process.

Historical literature has practically not touched upon the subject of how the settlement policy in Russia was worked out, or how it was based on the experiences of other European countries. References to "enlightened absolutism" alone are insufficient. There was a concrete historical practice which served as a model for the Russian government.⁶¹

By the time Catherine II came to the throne the leading European states (Great Britain and France) had a practice of colonization policy developed when populating the North American colonies. This policy was based on rather harsh principles. The settlers had to pay a considerable sum of money to cover transportation costs, and those unable to pay on arrival became "contract workmen." From the day the first colony was founded in Jamestown and up to the revolution of 1776 (and in some places even fifty years after) it was a routine practice in the British colonies that white immigrants were turned into virtual slaves for a period of seven years and sometimes longer to repay the cost of ocean

---

⁶⁰ Eighteenth century religious denominations that opposed the official Russian Orthodox Church were persecuted for disobedience to the authorities and refusal to serve in the army; they migrated to Canada at the end of the nineteenth century.
⁶¹ *Ocherki istorii nemtsev i mennonitov*, Bobyleva, 24.

crossing. Civil and criminal law placed them on the same footing as slaves. Prior to 1700 more than half of the immigrants in Virginia had been "contract workmen."[62]

However, the Russian Empress chose to follow the colonization policy of the Prussian rulers of the seventeenth to eighteenth centuries. Her Manifesto of 1763 basically copied the Potsdam Edict of 1684 of the Great Elector Frederick William, with only a handful of separate clauses being extended and developed.[63]

Despite some shortcomings when implementing the principles of Catherine II's manifesto, it did not lose its significance and constituted the basis of Russian legislation regarding foreign colonists. The responsibility for the settlement was placed on the Office for Foreigners' Guardianship which was founded almost at the same time the as the manifesto of 1763 was issued, and put under the direct control of Catherine II herself. The Empress's favorite, Count Grigorii Orlov, was appointed head of *Kantseliariia*. The instructions outlining the responsibilities of the Office said that its main task was to provide favorable conditions for the resettling colonists.[64] The Office should make an inventory of the property brought by the settlers, compile maps of vacant land, and make sure that the newcomers were properly settled.[65]

On Orlov's initiative an "Instruction about the delimitation of lands allotted for settling foreign colonists" was published in March 1764. The document appointed land-surveyors to delimit the boundaries of future colonies, with the assistance of personnel hand-picked from military detachments. On the same day, "Rules for Colonies" were issued, which were to regulate life in the colonies. On 22 March 1764, there appeared a "Plan for Populating New Russia province," which was a kind of supplement to the 1763 manifesto. The plan was an attempt to embrace all aspects of life in the region and to adjust them to the demands of colonization. It became a law that remained in force in New Russia until the 1780s.[66] The Catherinean law put foreign colonists on a privileged footing compared to the other tax-payers in the Russian Empire. Foreigners were granted big lots of arable land on communal property

---

[62] William Foster, *Ocherki politicheskoi istorii Ameriki* (Moskva, 1955), 115–116.
[63] *Ocherki istorii nemtsev i mennonitov*, Bobyleva, 27–28.
[64] Iakov Ditz, *Istoriia povolzhskikh nemtsev-kolonistov* (Moskva: Gotika, 1997), 39–40.
[65] Klaus, *Nashi kolonii*, 15.
[66] Natalia Polonska-Vasylenko, "Pivdenna Ukraina 1787 (zi studii istorii kolonizatsii)," in *Zaporizhzhia 18 stolittia ta iogo spadshchyna*, t. 2 (Munich: Dniprova khvylia, 1967), 136.

and individual land tenure. The Swedes who resettled not as foreigners but as Russian subjects nevertheless obtained land, tax privileges, means for building and starting a home of their own, sowing grain, provisions at public expense for the first year etc. It is clear, therefore, that on the legislative level the Russian authorities treated colonists and the Swedes with consideration and benevolence.

However, the governmental orders were not always carried out because of the circumstances and the specific mentality of Russian bureaucrats. All the more so, when in 1782 the Office for Foreigners' Guardianship was abolished and the Swedes on arrival in the Kherson region were left with no assistance in settling their affairs. Such assistance had previously been given to foreign resettlers in other regions – to a greater or lesser degree.

Paul I intended to raise the social and cultural level of the colonies, making them into model households. He demanded impartial information as to the state of the colonies. In March 1797 he established a special department tasked with assisting the foreign colonists in the development of agriculture – the Board of State Economy, Guardianship of Foreigners and Rural Husbandry.[67]

In 1798 Court Adviser Samuel Contenius was sent to New Russia to assess the situation and inform the government about the state of affairs in the colonies. Contenius was also expected to suggest improvements. The authorities were particularly worried by the situation that had appeared in the Swedish and Danzig colonies. Contenius was asked, in particular, to evaluate the general situation in those colonies, the conditions of life and work of the Swedes, and also of the privileges they had been given. He was also instructed to gather information concerning public expenses in those colonies and find out what taxes they paid to the state.[68]

The information presented by Samuel Contenius formed the basis of the Senate report of 6 April 1800. The report suggested improvements in the conditions of New Russia's foreign settlers, and set up an institution

---

[67] PSZRI, sobr. 1, t. 24, no. 17865.
[68] Law – applying to all or large groups of population. In our context privilege means full or partial exemption from laws.

for supporting the colonists – the Guardianship Office of New Russian Foreign Settlers of Southern Russia.[69]

The report characterized the twenty-two families of Swedes as "zealous and hardworking in farming and house-keeping." However, crop yields were poor because of the unfortunate colony location and the climate of the region. In order to make ends meet, they[70] "engaged in fishing which was their primary source of income." The report proposed that, with all things considered, the Swedes ought to be given the status of colonists as "they were resettled from a far-off land, with a different climate, and placed among people differing from them in their customs, faith and language."[71] This proposal was confirmed by the Emperor. Another no less important step taken by Paul I was to approve the "Instructions to the Guardianship Office" of 26 July 1800 and the "Instructions for regulations and management of colonies" of 16 May 1801. The clauses of the Instructions show that their aim was to create the instruments necessary for managing the colonies and improving living conditions there. During Alexander I's reign good guardianship was provided for the development of colonies. He continued the work that his father, Paul I, had begun. Among the institutions formed to reform Russia, the Committee for the Development of New Russia (further – Committee), held a prominent place.[72] The Committee started its work in December 1801. Though it did not produce any significant documents concerning colonists, the very fact of its existence proved the government's concern about the region's urgent problems including those of the colonists. In 1802, Ministries replaced Collegia and the control over the colonies passed to the Ministry of the Interior. Local branches of the Guardianship Office were subordinated to that Ministry. Without going into details concerning a new order issued in February 1804 – "About receiving and settling foreign colonists" – it should be noted that it marked the beginning of a new stage of foreign colonization and its main task was to stimulate the economic development of the recently populated territories.[73]

---

[69] *O predlagaemykh sredstvakh k popravleniu sostoianiia Novorossiiskikh inostrannykh poselentsev i ob uchrezhdenii pod vedomstvom Ekspeditsii gosudarstvennogo khoziaistva, Kontory opekunstva Novorossiiskikh inostrannykh poselentsev.*
[70] Iakov Ditz, *Istoriia povolzhskikh nemtsev-kolonistov* (Moskva: Gotika, 1997), 39–40.
[71] PSZRI, sobr. 1, t. 26, str.115–128.
[72] In Russian: Komitet ob ustroenii Novorossiiskoi gubernii.
[73] *O priiome i vodvorenii inostrannykh kolonistov.*

Owing to the growing number of colonists and the plans of the government, the bodies managing the colonies were reorganized in 1818. A state committee was established called the Trustees Committee for Foreign Settlers in Southern Russia for the southern territories including Ekaterinoslav, Odessa and Bessarabia departments. These structures were placed under Ivan Inzov, the Chief Guardian of the colonists of New Russia. The most important functions of these departments were supervision of the economic development of the colonies, auditing of the public funding for the colonists, control of the colonists' doing their duty, etc.

These departments were abolished in 1833 as a result of a new policy; there were to be no more settlements of foreign colonists and free entry into Russia was no longer allowed. In 1842, many different legislative acts concerning foreign colonists were replaced with one set of "Regulations for the Colonies."[74] In 1857, "Regulations Concerning Foreigners' Colonies in the Empire" were issued by the authorities.[75] This document contained the bulk of the information accumulated by the Russian government concerning the legal status of the foreign colonies. Its nine sections and 577 clauses covered, in minute detail, the colonists' rights and obligations, the system of managing the colonies, and the rules governing the life of the foreign colonists.[76] There was considerable variation between different groups of colonists, e.g. with regard to the size of land lots, terms of paying all debts, and period of privileged years. The rules applying to the Swedes were listed in legislation concerning German colonists which could probably be explained by the geographical position of their settlements. German colonists and the Swedes were in a more privileged position as compared with Bulgarians, Montenegrins, Serbs, and Italians.

An important factor in the life of the colonists in general and the Swedish colonists in particular was that the people who managed the colonization process were close to the throne, and enjoyed great authority and the full confidence of the ruler. Last but not least, they did not merely carry out the Tsar's decrees, but also took initiatives on their own to bring about change and they were talented organizers. Among them, one can mention Grigorii Potemkin, Samuel Contenius, Emmanuel

---

[74] "Ustav o koloniiakh inostrantsev v Imperii," in *Svod zakonov Rossiiskoi imperii*, t. 12, ch. 2 (Sankt-Peterburg: Tip.2 Otdeleniia s.e.i.v. kantseliarii, 1857).
[75] Ustav o koloniiakh.
[76] Ustav o koloniiakh inostrantsev v Imperii.

Richelieu, Johan Kornis, Platon Zubov, and Ivan Inzov.[77] Contemporary judgments of them ranged from blind admiration to bitter criticism.

Documents in archives and the correspondence of the leading personalities show that their attitude towards the Swedish colonists was one of sympathy. Samuel Contenius compiled trustworthy and balanced information about them, and his proposals for improving their situation became the basis for granting them the status of colonists. In his capacity as main moderator of the Guardianship Office he became one of the key figures in the colonization process.[78] He made regular inspections and wrote reports on the situation in the colonies, including the Swedish colony.[79] He wrote the instructions on the duties of supervisors in the foreign colonies of Kherson and Tiraspol provinces,[80] inspected the bookkeeping work of the *Kontora opekunstva*,[81] and analyzed the specific conditions of nature and climate in the settlement territories.[82] He also tried to find ways to improve the colonists' economic conditions[83] by introducing new trades and sources of income such as sheep breeding, forestry, gardening, and silkworm breeding.[84] However, in these efforts, he was often forced to overcome initial resistance by the colonists. He also improved the medical service provided to the colonists and he took charge of smallpox vaccination among them. Contenius provided for the expansion of arable farming[85] and solved a number of controversial issues.[86]

Conclusions

In the second half of the eighteenth century, the Russian state regarded the colonization of New Russia as the most important aspect of its policy, both from an economic and a strategic point of view. The Russian monarchs (Catherine II, Paul I, Alexander I and to some extent, Nikolai I too) paid great attention to settlement policy and the popu-

---

[77] Bagalei, *Kolonizatsiia Novorossiiskogo kraia*, 112.
[78] Glavnyi Sudia.
[79] DAOO, f. 1, op. 220, spr. 4, arkk.122–126.
[80] DAOO, f. 1, op. 1, spr. 969, arkk.114–124.
[81] DAOO, f. 1, op. 1, spr. 215, arkk. 24–25.
[82] DAOO, f. 1, op. 220, spr. 4, arkk. 122–126.
[83] RGIA, f. 383, op. 29, d. 199, ll.1–3.
[84] DAOO, f. 6, op. 1, spr. 969, arkk. 100–110; DADO, f. 134, op. 1, spr. 428, arkk. 29–42.
[85] DAOO, f. 252, op. 1, spr.10, ark. 4.
[86] DAOO, f.6, op. 1, spr. 281, ark.1.

lating of the Wild Field territories. This becomes apparent both from the orders they issued to regulate the regional conditions, and from their personal correspondence.

A number of factors can explain the hardships experienced by the Estonian Swedes during their initial years in their new settlement. The Russian administration had no experience of colonization, as the Swedes were the first colonists in this region. They could not benefit from the experiences of predecessors – there were none. The route taken by the Swedes was too long, and the season of the year – fall was not suitable for such a long journey. At the time of their migration, the Russian officials had little knowledge of the natural and climatic conditions in the area where the Swedes were to settle.

The interrelation of the Swedish population in Kherson province and the Russian state should be viewed in the general context of the colonization policy in the region. Two important questions are: How many families left Dagö to settle in Ukraine, and when was the colony founded? They are directly connected with the land problem that arose many years later. The problem of land tenure and of military service was connected with legislation for all of Russia. Therefore, one cannot speak of a breach of rights and a betrayal of the privileges of the Swedes by the Russian state. A noble part in the life of the Swedish colonists was played by people who were directly in charge of the colonization process in the region (Grigorii Potemkin, Emmanuel Richelieu, Samuel Contenius, and Ivan Inzov).

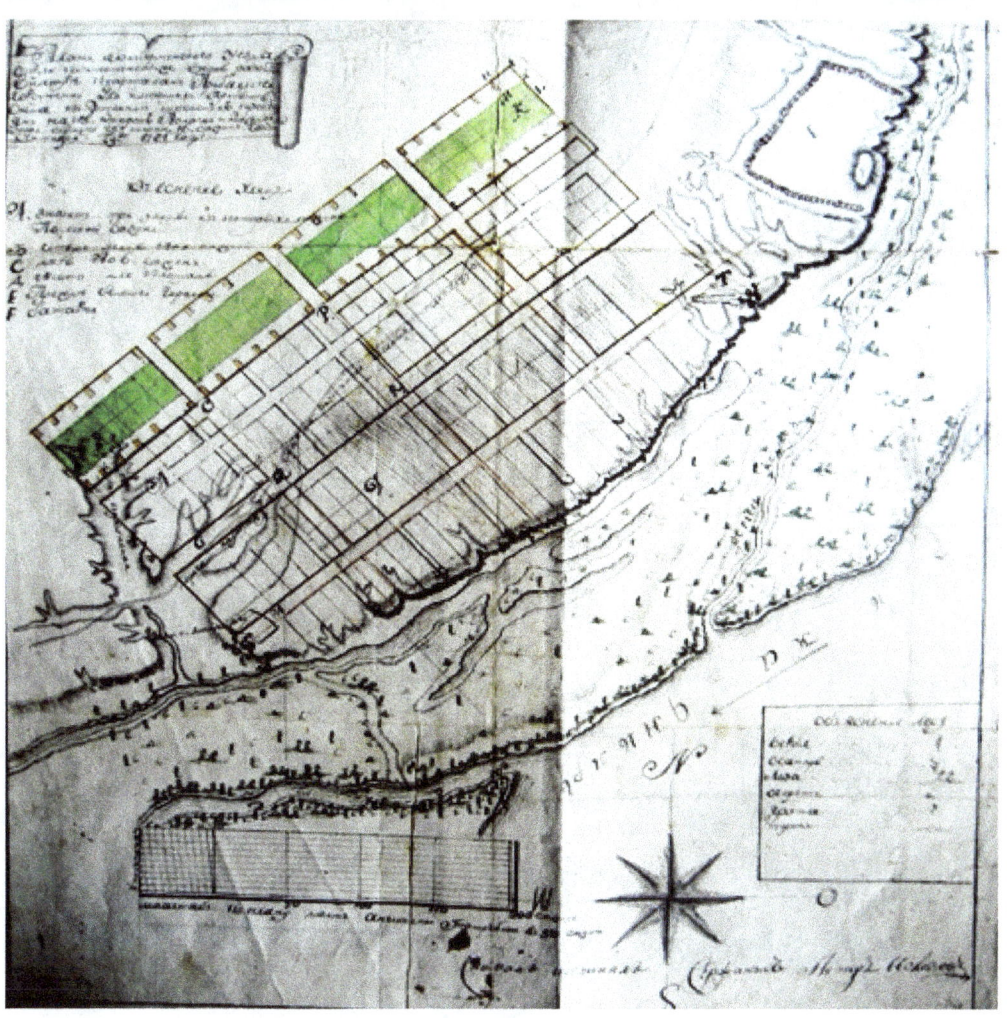

Map 6: Grand plan, poor outcome. A project map of the future Swedish colony made in 1781, with the village (township?) neatly divided into farmsteads and streets.
Plan of Kazykermen [Kezikermen] district of Kazykermen province divided into lots for Swedish peasants from Estonia. It planned for 105 dvors, supposed to be 25 sazhens in length and 16 sazhens in width for each dvor. The Plan was constituted on 19 September 1781. DAKhO, f. 14, op.1, spr.85, ark.13.

Map 7: *Ethnographic Map of the Russian Empire*, 1851 ("Etnograficheskaia karta Rossiiskoi Imperii").
The light blue colour that signifies Swedes is hard to find, surrounded as it is by red colour for Germans (Klosterdorf and Mühlhausendorf) and black colour for Jews. A darker shade of blue colour signifies Tatars. For safety's sake, the publishers kindly awarded each group a number – 37 for Swedes, 23 for Germans, 10 for Jews and 29 for Tatars. Krigsarkivet, 0403/31/A/027c.

People in between
– Baltic islanders as colonists on the steppe

JULIA MALITSKA

This shapter deals with the acculturation of the Estonian Swedes in New Russia during the period 1805–1871. It is divided into three main parts. The first part highlights the social-economic activity of the Estonian Swedes in New Russia, their role in the colonization of the Black and Azov Sea region. The second part deals with the relations between the Swedes and their neighbors. The final part of the chapter describes the culture of the Swedish colonists, the process of their acculturation and integration into a new cultural and social milieu, and gives an outline of their special identity.

The Estonian Swedes became agents of Russia's colonization project in the Black and Azov Sea region unintentionally; their migration was not spontaneous, but undertaken as a result of planning by the authorities and with their support. On a propaganda mission among the Dagö Swedes in the summer of 1781, Russian officials, in particular Colonel Ivan Sinelnikov, created an image of New Russia as a prosperous land. When the Swedes arrived at their destination, there was a clash between that image and the reality of the region. In the first few years in the new settlement, nature and climate in combination with various social factors wrought havoc among the settlers, causing a drastic decline in their numbers. Therefore, their adaptation took an extremely long time, about 20–25 years, (1782–1805/1807), compared to the average adaptation period of 8–10 years.[1]

---

[1] Leonid Rybakovskii, *Migratsiia naseleniia. Tri stadii migratsionnogo protsessa (Ocherki teorii i metodov issledovaniia)* (Moskva: Nauka, 2001), 91.

During these 20–25 years, the Estonian Swedes adapted to new climatic conditions and overcame the demographic catastrophe which threatened the existence of Gammalsvenskby. Although the birth rate was high, the population grew only slowly because of the high child mortality. Slow but more or less stable population growth started in 1795–1796.[2]

Figure 1: The Size of the Population of Gammalsvenskby 1781–1929.

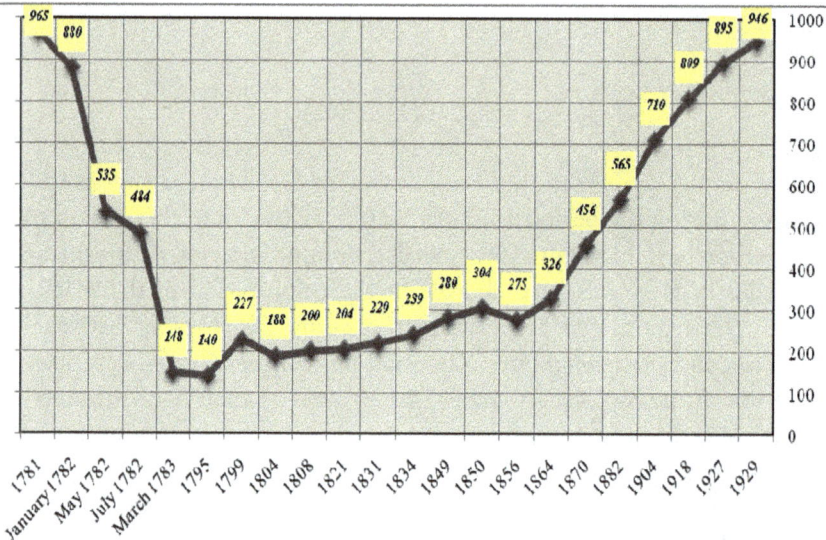

Source: Julia Malitska, *Estonski shvedy na Pivdni Rosiiskoi imperii: mihratsiia, adaptatsiia ta aculturatsiia pereselentsiv-colonistiv (1781–1871)* [*The Estonian Swedes in the South of the Russian Empire: Migration, Adaptation and Acculturation of the Migrants-Colonists (1781–1871)*], Manuscript of the Candidate thesis (Dnipropetrovsk, 2010), 242.

The building of a church and permanent dwellings, the first attempts in agriculture and, finally, the attainment of the status of colonists signified the end of the accommodation and adaptation period, as well as a certain measure of legal integration. Furthermore, in 1804–1805, the Swedish village became a board centre and an administrative unit of New Russia.

---

[2] DADO, f. 134, op. 1, spr. 204, ark. 13; *Gammalsvenskbydokument*, Alexander Loit & Nils Tiberg (Uppsala: Lundequistska bokh., 1958), 42, 115–146.

The long accommodation process of the Estonian Swedes in New Russia is explained by the following factors. The government's colonization plans were risky and adventurous; therefore an improved resettlement strategy, efficient support, and guarantees of emigration conditions for Swedes were absent. The Russian government in St Petersburg and its diplomatic agents abroad were not aware of the actual climatic conditions and the geographic specifics of the recently annexed steppe of the Black Sea region. As a result, the Swedes were unintentionally misinformed about the region where they were to settle, which made the cultural and psychological shock when they arrived acute. Their spontaneous decision to move to a new place, the lack of adequate information about the region they had come to meant that they had little opportunity to work out new strategies and find ways to cope with the difficult conditions of the steppe. The distance between their old home on Dagö and the new settlement was huge and so was the difference between the living conditions of the two places. The physical exhaustion of the migrants, the disastrous mortality among them during 1782–1783[3] and the resulting breakup of families meant that there was little population growth in the ensuing years and that the Swedes had difficulties in adjusting to the new place. Owing to bad timing and misunderstandings between the Russian government and the local colonist administration they reacted too slowly to the housing problems, food shortages and other hardships suffered by Swedes. Finally, the age structure of the Swedish colonist group – many were children – caused problems for their social and economic adjustment and made their community vulnerable to external developments.[4]

Theoretical remarks

One can question whether, or how far, modern theories of adaptation and acculturation are applicable to the migrations and resettlements of the eighteenth and nineteenth centuries. Be that as it may, such theories

---

[3] DAOO, f. 6, op. 1, spr. 65, arkk. 104, 119, 123; *Gammalsvenskbydokument*, Loit & Tiberg, 38, 43, 147–164; Alexander Loit, "Pereselenie shvedov iz Estonii na Ukrainu v kontse 18 veka," in *Skandinavskii sbornik*, no. 32 (Tallinn: Eesti paamat, 1988), 112–114.

[4] Julia Malitska, *Estonski shvedy na Pivdni Rosiiskoi imperii: mihratsiia, adaptatsiia ta aculturatsiia pereselentsiv-colonistiv (1781–1871)[The Estonian Swedes in the South of the Russian Empire: Migration, Adaptation and Acculturation of the Migrants-Colonists (1781–1871)]*, Manuscript of the Candidate thesis (Dnipropetrovsk, 2010), 77–115.

are stimulating and inspiring, and although this chapter primarily aims at presenting empirical material, some of the theoretical ideas the author had in mind when analyzing her sources will be presented here.

As a result of acculturation, changes occur both on the individual and on the group level. The direct interaction of groups of individuals, who belong to different cultures, leads to changes in the primary cultural codes of one or several groups. On the group level, several changes may occur. To begin with, the newcomers are faced with a new place of residence, with (for them) unusual agricultural and climatic conditions along with different population density. They also face a different biological milieu with new food, unknown diseases etc. In addition, there are usually legal changes, when the non-dominant groups get under the control of the major groups and lose some of their autonomy. To another category of changes one can count the economic ones that cause modifications in the traditional activities and management forms. Finally, there are cultural transformations that influence the traditional language, religious codes within the intergroup, but also interpersonal relations. As will be shown, the Swedes as a group were facing all of the above.

In a multicultural environment, both individuals and groups face two main problems. The first problem is connected with one's identity and how it is manifested. In this connection, the question arises whether the individual or group at all chooses to emphasize and preserve its ethnic originality or not. The second problem is whether the individuals and groups wish to stress the contrast with other ethnic groups. In this context, it is necessary to define if the relations with major ethnic groups are viewed as desirable.[5] Obviously, in everyday interaction, groups and individuals can either preserve the cultural codes and maintain the cultural originality, or go for contact and participation in the wider society, thus joining other cultural groups.[6]

Following John Berry's terminology, the four major patterns of interethnic encounters are assimilation, separation, integration, and marginalization. Particularly, interethnic integration covers the preserving of a certain cultural integrity of a group, as well as an intention of becoming an

---

[5] John Berry, "Akkulturatsiia i psikhologicheskaia adaptatsiia: obzor problemy (nachalo)," *Razvitie lichnosti*, no. 3–4 (2001):183–193; John Berry, "Akkulturatsiia i psikhologicheskaia adaptatsiia: obzor problemy (okonchanie)," *Razvitie lichnosti*, no.1 (2002), 291–296.

[6] Elvira Plesskaia, "Problemy sokhraneniia natsionalnoi kultury v usloviiakh sushchestvovaniia i vzaimodeistviia s kulturoi titulnoi natsii," in *Kliuchevye problemy istorii rossiiskikh nemtsev* (Moskva: MSNK-press, 2004), 192–204.

integral part of the society (adaptability). Hence, the cultural identity and originality are preserved even though the group chooses to become a part of the dominant society. With a development of this pattern, several different groups cooperate within the major social system. As a result of the integration pattern, selective acceptance of behavior moulds between the interacting groups occurs. According to Berry, interethnic integration demands from the ethnic groups and national minorities the gradual adaptation to the main values of the dominant society, which in turn should adapt its social institutions (education, administration etc.) to the needs of the multicultural society. The non-dominant groups achieve voluntary integration successfully only when the dominant society is open and aspiring to cultural variety. A crucial factor is that both groups recognize the other group's right to exist as a distinct people.[7] There are two main factors of intercultural adaptation: the first one is the width of the cultural distance between the interacting groups; the other contains the peculiarities of the culture of the migrants, and the culture prevalent at the place of their new settlement.

The migrants might suffer "cultural shock" in their new country or place of residence. The culture of a new country or region of settlement compels the migrants to partly or completely give up their former way of life, which requires socio-cultural adaptation. Thus, there are three main factors involved in successful socio-cultural adaptation: establishing positive contacts with the new neighbors, solving everyday issues, and participating in the socio-cultural life of a new society. The main factor that determines the socio-cultural adaptation process is the distance between the migrant's native culture and the culture of the new place of settlement (including language, religion, climatic and diet differences).[8]

Due to the official origin of sources used in this study, the author focuses on the adaptation and acculturation of the Swedes on the group level.

---

[7] John Berry, "Acculturation," in *Joan E. Grusec, Paul D. Hastings, Handbook of Socialization: Theory and Research* (New York: The Guilford Press, 2006), 543; John Berry, "Acculturation," in *Joan E. Grusec, Paul D. Hastings, Handbook of Socialization: Theory and Research* (New York: The Guilford Press, 2006), 550–552.
[8] Tatiana Stefanenko, *Etnopsikhologiia* (Moskva: Institut psikhologii RAN," Akademicheskii proekt," 1999), 164–165.

The Swedish colonists' economy: anglers or farmers?

According to the Russian imperial vision, the annexed Black and Azov Sea territories were to be developed as part of the agricultural infrastructure. Therefore, the encouragement of farming among the colonists and peasants was one of the main tasks of the government of the region. Among several top-down agricultural projects was the breeding of cattle. The colonist administration[9] was particularly encouraged by the report of the Minister of the Interior, which was approved by the Senate in 1806, on the need to promote cattle and horse breeding on the lands between Buh and Dnister rivers.[10] Thus, despite a certain measure of skepticism among the Swedish colonists, they became a part of grand "agricultural projects" of the colonist administration in the region.[11]

Farming among the Swedes was of course heavily influenced by the natural geographic and climatic conditions, the availability of water and by the special background of the settlers and the skills they brought with them. Another important factor was the colonist administration. The relations of the Swedish colonists with the colonist administration were wide-ranging. The sources used here do not support the idea that the Russian government was hostile to the Swedish colonists and deceived them.[12] They reveal a considerable degree of irresponsibility, and unsatisfactory coordination between the central power and the colonist administration, rather than a prejudiced attitude towards the Swedish colonists. However, the Swedes merely constituted one group among many. Recent scholarship on Russian imperial history has described Russia's bureaucracy and "differentiated governance" as a way of ruling heterogeneous imperial space.[13]

---

[9] Here, the term encompasses the Guardianship Office of New Russian Foreign Settlers of Southern Russia, later on – the Trustees Committee for Foreign Settlers in Southern Russia.
[10] *Polnoe sobranie zakonov Rossiiskoi imperii.* Tom 29 (1806–1807) (St Petersburg, 1830), 785–787.
[11] *Samuil Khristianovich Contenius ob inostrannoi kolonizatsii Iuzhnoi Rossii, sbornik dokumentov 1801–1829*, ed. Olga Eisfeld (Odessa: Astroprint, 2003), 13; DAOO, f.6, op. 2, spr. 4460, arkk. 1–2.
[12] Hanna Chumachenko, "Shvedske poselennia na pivdni Ukrainy," *Narodna tvorchist ta etnografiia*, no. 2–3 (1997), 101–110; Loit, "Pereselenie shvedov," 104–116.
[13] From enormous amount of literature see: *Russian Empire: Space, People, Power, 1700–1930*, ed. Jane Burbank, Mark von Hagen, and Anatolyi Remnev (Indiana University Press, 2007).

Document 3: The fragment of Emmanuel Richelieu's letter to Samuel Contenius, 9 April 1806.

> /.../ The settlers of the Swedish colony ask for some assistance in finishing their houses. I consider this request quite reasonable, as there was only one carpenter among them, which is insufficient to teach others. Therefore they had to hire a Russian carpenter for 12 and 15 Rubles per house. The houses there are only partly built, as they have no money to finish them.

Source: Pisma gertsoga Armana Emmanuila de Richelieu Samuilu Khristianovichu Conteniusu 1803–1814, ed. Olga Konovalova (Odessa: OKFA "TES," 1999), 99.

Starting from the beginning of the nineteenth century, the colonist administration took the following steps to improve the situation of the Swedes. It made a financial contribution to the rebuilding of the Gammalsvenskby church and finishing of the Swedish houses.[14] Moreover, the colonist administration introduced sanitary, and quarantine measures against epidemics in the Swedish district. One such case was the isolation from neighboring villages in order to prevent the cholera epidemics (1837). Another case was the routine vaccination of the Swedish children against smallpox etc.[15] The administration often supported the Swedish colonists with food supplies and it also provided the Swedes with seed for sowing, or money to purchase grain and food in times of poor harvests, thus preventing famine and economic decline.[16] Additional financial assistance was provided by the state to the head of each household personally when needed, and particularly in cases of lack of food reserves during unusually severe winters.[17]

Document 4: Samuel Contenius report to governor-general Emmanuel Richelieu about the lack of bread in Molochna, Swedish and Odessa colonies and in this connection paying food money to the colonists. Odessa, 17 November 1806

> Your Excellency, Sir Emmanuel Osipovich!
>
> From the reports of the caretaker of colonies I found out, that Molochna colonists and the colonists newly settled down in

---

[14] DAOO, f. 6, op. 1, spr. 128, arkk. 9, 17-22, 24-26; DADO, f. 134, op. 1, spr. 102, arkk. 10–13.
[15] DAOO, f. 6, op. 1, spr. 195, ark. 167.
[16] *Samuil Khristianovich Contenius,* Eisfeld, 177–178, 205–208.
[17] *Samuil Khristianovich Contenius,* Eisfeld, 176.

the Swedish colony because of the poor harvest do not have enough bread for livelihood during winter. During the inspection of the colonies settled down nearby Odessa, I have also noticed a considerable lack of bread. For the sake of non-starvation I recognize the need to continue paying 5 kopecks of food money per day to each person as long as necessary. Thereby I ask the permission of Your Excellency.

Note: Richelieu has agreed with Contenius proposition, but with one clause: those who have enough bread for winter, are not paid food money.
Source: Samuil Khristianovich Contenius ob inostrannoi kolonizatsii Iuzhnoi Rossii, sbornik dokumentov 1801–1829, ed. Olga Eisfeld (Odessa: Astroprint, 2003), 176.

Along with other colonists of the region, the Swedes were encouraged to engage in pet "agricultural projects" of the colonist administration such as forestry, cattle breeding, sericulture, tobacco growing, dam building, and digging of the wells.[18]

The humid tropical heat of the region combined with the long drought in summer was frequently followed by cold winters (even colder than on Dagö, where snow was rather common). The fields of the Swedes were often flooded in spring, then there was drought, and there were hot dry winds from the steppe, people were struck down by epidemics of scurvy, cholera, typhus, and rodents and locusts ate the crops. The extreme weather conditions of the steppe were intensified by severe and snowy winters, extremely hot summers with hurricanes and hail, that often made Swedes and other colonists helpless.[19] Being located on a hill, the Swedish colony suffered dearth of water resources. The fields were heavily exposed to the sun, which stimulated the burning-out of the harvests.

In the 1840s, a new project – the creation of artificial lakes in order to preserve the melting water from the spring floods, and thus to have the water resources required for cattle breeding for a whole year – was launched. At the time, recurring drought in the region gave further impetus to this project. The Swedes and the Khortitsa Mennonites responded positively to the government's initiative to build a dam between

---

[18] Jan Utas, *Svenskbyborna. Historia och öde från trettonhundra till nu* (Visby: Gotlands Allehandas Förlag, 1982), 71.
[19] DAOO, f. 6, op. 1, spr. 5140, arkk. 5–39; Elena Druzhynina, *Iuzhnaia Ukraina (1800–1825)* (Moskva: Nauka, 1970), 228-229; DADO, f.134, op. 1, spr. 784,789; *Ocherki istorii nemtsev i mennonitov Iuga Ukrainy (konets 18 – pervaia polovina 19 vekov)*, ed. Svetlana Bobyleva (Dnipropetrovsk: Art-Press, 1999), 61.

Gammalsvenskby and the neighboring German village of Klosterdorf. This would make it possible to flood the land in the spring in order to facilitate cattle breeding.[20]

Military campaigns also affected life in the Swedish colony. For instance, during the Russian-Turkish wars of 1828–1829 and 1836–1837 and the Crimean war 1853–1856, Russian units passed the Swedish settlement, infecting its inhabitants with cholera and typhus.[21]

Before their migration to New Russia, the majority of the Dagö Swedes was engaged in fishing, cattle breeding and livestock production. Since they had now settled in a locality that was not very suitable for agriculture, and since steppe farming was unknown to them, good harvests were not to be expected.

Eventually, the Swedish peasants learned to plough according to local custom, hitching four pairs of oxen to the plough. During their pioneer decades on the steppe, the Swedes ploughed their land with a *ralo,* the traditional wooden plough of the region.[22] Later, it was replaced with the German colonists' *bukker* with iron blades.[23] They grew rye, spring and winter grains (for making bread), barley, flax, millet, watermelon and melon.[24] However, the grains were grown only with great difficulty, even when local farming techniques were used. In order to support the inhabitants in times of poor grain harvests and to prevent famine among them, granaries were built in the colonies of the Swedish district. In 1819, the granary of Gammalsvenskby contained more reserves of grain than the other two in the district: 59 per cent of the rye reserves and 57 per cent of spring bread reserves.[25] Despite the Swedish colonists' diligence in agriculture, their food needs were hardly satisfied, primarily because of the extreme climate of the region.

In order to improve the economic situation of the Swedes, the Guardianship Office initiated an experiment in 1817. They were encouraged to grow Hungarian tobacco, a cash crop. Eventually, the colonists were successful, and tobacco was continuously cultivated in the village.[26]

---

[20] *Ocherki istorii nemtsev i mennonitov,* Bobyleva, 107; Utas, *Svenskbyborna,* 78.
[21] Utas, *Svenskbyborna,* 72–75; Hedman, *Gammalsvenskby – the true story.*
[22] *Ralo* is Ukrainian for a type of a plough.
[23] *Materialy dlia otsenki zemel Khersonskoi gubernii,* t. 6. Khersonskii uezd (Kherson: Tip. O.D. Khodushynoi, 1890), 222–223, 226.
[24] DAOO, f. 6, op. 1, spr. 4935, arkk. 2–13; spr. 269, arkk. 6–26.
[25] DADO, f. 134, op. 1, spr. 579, ark. 8.
[26] DADO, f. 134, op. 1, spr. 512, arkk. 2–22.

According to the governmental instruction of 26 July 1800, the Guardianship Office should have encouraged the foreign colonists to plant grass to create pastures, to plant mulberry trees, grapevines, sesame seeds and other useful plants.[27] For every sixty to eighty *desiatinas* of land the Swedish colonists were obliged to plant half a *desiatina* with trees. The aim was to create more favorable conditions for the development of agriculture, but also to protect the land from the hot dry steppe winds and from drifting snow in the winter. The trees were planted on special plots close to the church and the district centre, and on the land surrounding the colonists' households.

Every farmer who had received seedlings from the colonist administration was obliged to plant a certain number of trees near his house.[28] The colonists of the Swedish district were successful in the cultivation of acacia, which, beginning in the 1830s, was cultivated on the common land of the villagers.[29] Pussy willow, elderberry, and sedge, which mainly had a decorative function, were planted on the colonists' homestead lands. The climate in the Kherson province was not favorable for oak, maple, and birch, thus they did not take root.[30] Unfortunately, despite the colonist administration's support and promotion, viticulture did not develop satisfactorily and the produce did not suffice even for the needs of the colonists.[31]

As to horticulture and vegetable gardening, the Swedish colonists did not believe they could succeed in it because of the location of their village, on a hill with hot summer winds.[32] However, the colonist administration promoted the foundation of communal plantations and nurseries in Gammalsvenskby to cultivate fruit trees. Occasionally, the Guardianship Office supplied the model farmers among the Swedes with fruit tree seedlings from Kursk province.[33] Eventually, gardens with apple-trees, plum-trees, apricot-trees, cherry-trees, pear-trees blossomed

---

[27] *Materialy dlia otsenki zemel Khersonskoi gubernii*, 148; *Nemtsy v istorii Rossii: dokumenty vysshykh organov vlasti i voennogo komandovaniia, 1652–1917*, ed. Viktor Diesendorf (Moskva: MFD: Materik, 2006), 95.

[28] DAOO, f. 6, op. 1, spr. 5137, arkk. 1-2; Wilhelm Lagus, "Utflygt till Dniepern i April 1852," *Finlands Allmänna Tidning*, no.132(1852), 549.

[29] DADO, f. 134, op. 1, spr. 868, ark. 5; spr. 579, ark. 13.

[30] DAOO, f. 6, op. 1, spr. 4460, ark. 2.

[31] *Samuil Khristianovich Contenius*, Eisfeld, 261; DAOO, f.6, op. 1, spr. 2437.

[32] Lagus, "Utflygt till Dniepern," 549.

[33] *Samuil Khristianovich Contenius*, Eisfeld, 261.

in Gammalsvenskby. The cherry-trees yielded good harvests, whereas apricot-trees gave small and uncertain harvests.[34]

Together with neighboring colonists, the Swedish colonists were encouraged by the colonist administration to take up sericulture.[35] In summer 1815, a shed for silkworm growing was built in Gammalsvenskby paid by communal money.[36] However, the benefits of sericulture could not be reaped immediately. The sober-minded Samuel Contenius recognized that "this agricultural activity needed at least sixty to seventy years of persistent and hard work to get stable results and benefits."[37]

The breeding of cattle was an activity where the Swedish colonists had good chances for success. Free pasturelands were available which was important for the development of extensive cattle breeding. Moreover, the Swedes had former experience of cattle breeding from Estland where it dominated the economy.[38] With regard to the quantity of livestock, Estland held fourth place among Russia's European provinces. Sheep farming, pig farming and horse breeding were of secondary importance.[39] In this field, the Swedes had a clear advantage over other colonists. They proved able to adapt or rather rearrange their skills to a new climate and the terrain of the region.

By the beginning of the nineteenth century, a group of dedicated cattle breeders, (Hindrik Cristiansson, Hindrik Petersson, and Cristian Cristiansson) could be recognized.[40] From time to time, this agricultural activity proved vulnerable: 1810–1815, 1820–1825 and 1827 were the most difficult years. During this time, the livestock (horses, cows and sheep) was reduced significantly because of epidemics, diseases and poor harvests.[41] However, Gammalsvenskby still retained a leading position

---

[34] DADO, f.134, op. 1, spr. 579, ark. 13; spr. 868, ark. 5; spr. 202, arkk. 10–27; spr. 4460, ark. 2.
[35] DADO, f.134, op. 1, spr. 868, ark. 5; DAOO, f. 6, op. 1, spr. 4460, ark. 2.
[36] *Samuil Khristianovich Contenius*, Eisfeld, 263.
[37] *Samuil Khristianovich Contenius*, Eisfeld, 254.
[38] In 1719 the administrative absorbtion of the Baltic Sea region started: Estland was incorporated into the Russian Empire as a Reval province. It would only finally become known by its historical name, Estland province, in 1783.
[39] Karl Vrangel, "Estliandskaia guberniia," *Brockhaus and Efron Encyclopedic Dictionary*, accessed September 3, 2010, http://gatchina3000.ru/brockhaus-and-efron-encyclopedic-dictionary/119/119758.htm.
[40] DAOO, f. 6, op. 1, spr. 98, arkk. 138–139.
[41] Elena Druzhynina, *Iuzhnaia Ukraina (1800–1825)* (Moskva: Nauka, 1970), 213; *Ocherki istorii nemtsev i mennonitov*, Bobyleva, 74; DADO, f.134, op. 1, d. 784, l. 2; d. 868, l. 2.

among the villages of the Swedish district in large horned livestock (oxen, cows).[42]

Trade and natural carpentry, smithwork, shoemaking and weaving were the most widespread and popular handicrafts among the Swedish colonists.[43] As a home industry, weaving was the most popular among the Swedes of New Russia due to the availability of animal and plant raw materials, their former Dagö skills and experience. Almost every Swedish household had a spinning wheel for the production of linen.[44] Weaving was mostly based on wool, silk and flax fibers. It was the main handicraft of the Swedes prior to the village fire in 1835, when all spinning wheels brought from Dagö were consumed by the flames.[45]

Fishery and hunting were the salvation of the Swedish colonists in times of poor harvests. They were very skilful anglers and successful at selling what they caught. They had previous experience of fishing, from Dagö, and they learned new fishing methods from the Zaporizhian Cossacks when the old ones did not work on the steppe. Fish was often a staple in their diet as harvests were always uncertain and prices of agricultural products fluctuated. With hoop nets, a long line and fishing-spears they caught carp and sturgeon as well as more common fishes.

Almost every Swede had special equipment for professional fishing like fishing nets, valves and boats.[46] There was a demand which they could meet and thus get an additional income; sometimes fishing was their main source of income. Therefore a Swedish fishing *artel*[47] was formed which paid tax to the board on its earnings and signed a contract with the colonist administration every sixth year which laid down their rights and obligations.[48] Those who did not join the *artel* could fish only for the needs of their families. The Swedes usually dried and salted the

---

[42] DADO, f.134, op. 1, spr. 979, ark. 4; DAOO, f. 6, op. 1, spr. 4459, ark. 28.
[43] DADO, f. 134, op. 1, spr. 139, arkk. 80,85, 87,90; spr. 868, ark. 3; DAOO, f. 6, op. 1, spr. 99, l. 91; spr. 4459, ark. 28; Anatolii Afanasiev-Chuzhbynskyi, *Podorozh u Pivdennu Rosiiu* (Dnipropetrovsk: Sich, 2005), 261.
[44] DAOO, f. 6, op. 1, spr. 98, arkk. 135–139; DADO, f. 134, op. 1, spr. 139, ark. 91; spr. 868, ark. 3; spr. 979, ark. 4.
[45] *Severnyi arkhiv: Zhurnal istorii, statistiki i puteshestvii*, no. 8 (1824) 64–67.
[46] Afanasiev-Chuzhbynskyi, *Podorozh u Pivdennu Rosiiu*, 258–259.
[47] Artel (Russian: артель, Ukrainian: артіль) is a general term for various cooperative associations in Russia and Ukraine. Historically, artels were semi-formal associa-tions for various enterprises: fishing, mining, commerce etc. Commonly artels were seasonal, worked far from home and lived as a commune. Payment for job done was distributed according to verbal agreements, usually in equal shares.
[48] DAOO, f. 6, op. 1, spr. 1821, arkk. 1–12; spr. 8366, arkk. 4–31.

fish, and sold it on the markets and fairs of the nearby towns of Kakhovka, Berislav, and Kherson.[49] Obviously, their success was due to the extreme popularity of fish among the Orthodox and Jewish population of the region, especially during Lent. However, in some years the fishing resulted in losses. Thus, for instance in 1812–1813 in Kherson province, all boats and fishing activity was under the strict control of the colonist administration because of the plague that spread from the Pivdennyi Buh River.[50]

From being anglers, tar and lime stock manufacturers on their home island of Dagö, the Estonian Swedes have mastered the basics of challenging steppe agriculture. Alongside with the adjustment of their skills in fishery, weaving and cattle breeding, the Swedes gained new skills in sericulture, tobacco growing and forestry, due to governmental promoting. However, despite being quite hard-working and prepared to adjust to the new economic conditions, the reputation of the Swedes as modernizing agriculturists was not comparable, for instance, to that of the German-speaking and Mennonite colonists who lived in the same region.

Contested among strangers

For newly settled migrants it is essential to establish mutually beneficial contacts with neighbors. From time to time the idea of returning to Dagö was mooted among the Swedes due to despair and physical exhaustion.[51] However, they had lost contact with Dagö Island. Instead, new contacts were established with neighbors in the region where they had settled down.

The Swedes were the first colonists in New Russia, but not the first inhabitants of the steppe. There was a unique ethnic and social milieu formed by Cossacks, Romanis, Nomads, Tatars, and religious dissenters from Central Russia.[52] Like the Estonian Swedes, the religious dissenters were newcomers, but the rest had established themselves there long ago and considered the steppe their home.

---

[49] Afanasiev-Chuzhbynskyi, *Podorozh u Pivdennu Rosiiu*, 259; Druzhynina, *Iuzhnaia Ukraina*, 325.
[50] Druzhynina, *Iuzhnaia Ukraina*, 304.
[51] See Jan Utas, *Svenskbyborna*, 54–55.
[52] Iaroslav Boiko, Nataliia Danylenko, "Formuvannia etnichnogo skladu naselennia Pivdennoi Ukrainy (kinets 19–20 st.)," *Ukrainskyi istorychnyi zhurnal*, no. 9 (1992), 54–65.

The neighbors of the Swedes were Cossacks, Nomads, Spaniards and Greeks; Ukrainian and Russian peasants; German-speaking settlers. The Swedish population formed a specific community, which differed from the rest of the population in religion, language, type of dwellings, clothing, etc. At first, the Cossacks were not pleased with having neighbors on "their lands," and there even occurred some conflicts between them and the Swedes.[53] Nevertheless, the Cossacks were the first to help the Swedes adjust to the new conditions on the steppe. They provided the Swedes with some agricultural tools and instruments that could be used on virgin lands, and taught them practical skills in fishery and how to protect themselves from nomads. The Swedish-Cossack relations were quite ambiguous. On one hand, the Cossacks helped the Swedes to overcome the gravest initial problems, on the other hand, the Swedes from time to time had to protect themselves from being robbed by them.

Nomads caused the first colonists a lot of trouble. According to village oral tradition, Romanis looked for young Swedes to sell on the Crimean slave market. In winter 1787, Nogais attacked the Swedish village in an attempt to rob it. The priest Johan Adolph Europaeus fought back, and was injured when defending his family. Later, in 1788, because of the insecurity there, Europaeus left the village. The Swedes considered the Tatars to be the most honest and reliable people among their neighbors.[54] In the years 1783–1784, the Swedes got new neighbors. Groups of Spaniards and Greeks settled on their lands but there were no conflicts between the Swedes and these groups. Naturally, there were many Ukrainians and Russians among the neighbors of the Swedes. Russian religious dissenters from Moscow, Kaluga, Tula and Chernigov provinces were settled in Kherson region between 1752 and 1770, where they built large villages between the two rivers of Pivdennyi Buh and Dnipro.[55] The Swedes established commercial relations mainly with the local Ukrainians. The colonists hired local people from the neighboring town of Berislav as builders, carpenters, and shepherds, and they also bought timber from them. The Swedes also signed agreements concerning fishing rents with Ukrainians from the town of Berislav and Kiev province. The Swedish colonists were welcomed at Berislav and Kakhovka markets, since their traditional homemade cheese was very

---

[53] Utas, *Svenskbyborna*, 45.
[54] Utas, *Svenskbyborna*, 50–51.
[55] *Voenno-statisticheskoe obozrenie Rossiiskoi imperii, t. 11, ch. 1. Khersonskaia guberniia* (Sankt-Peterburg: Tip. Departamenta Gen. Shtaba, 1849), 85.

popular among the locals. After the fire in the village in 1835, the local Slavic population helped the Swedes to repair their roofs, having provided them with straw in exchange for fish.[56] There was also some contact between the Swedes and the Serbs.

Due to the decrease of the Swedish population during the first twenty years or so after their arrival, they were not able to cultivate all of the land granted to them by the Crown. Because of the growing shortage of land for colonization, the government decided to settle German-speaking migrants and Poles on Gammalsvenskby lands. Thus, in 1804, eight families of Danzig Poles were settled on land previously given to Swedes. The Swedes did not establish friendly contacts with the Catholic Poles.[57] Subsequently, the number of Poles was reduced; in 1830, after Andreas Maskewitsch's family had left the village, there was only one family left.

Not far from the Swedish village, 25 kilometers to the north of the colony, there was an Orthodox monastery called Grigorevskii Biziukov that gave assistance to the colonists in their agricultural activities. Towards the end of the nineteenth century, when the shortage of land made life particularly difficult, the Swedes were able to rent fertile land from the monastery on generous terms. Moreover, in the times of poor harvests, they were exempted from paying land rent by the Orthodox abbot.[58] In general, the relations between the Swedes and the Slavic population were well good. However, according to oral village tradition, the Swedish colonists were offended by "Russians" since they were considered to have installed Germans on the lands given to the Swedes by the Empress Catherine II.

Between 1804 and 1806 migrants from Bohemia, Austria, Württemberg, and Mainz on the Rhine, Baden, Prussia, Pomerania, Silesia and Palatinates established settlements, which were named Mühlhausendorf, Schlangendorf and Klosterdorf, on the sparsely populated "Swedish" lands. Most of them were Lutherans but there were also Catholic families among them. At the end of the eighteenth and the beginning of the nineteenth century, after constant, almost experimental, shuffles and reshuffles of the administration in the newly absorbed Azov and Black Sea territories, Gammalsvenskby, Mühl-

---

[56] Utas, *Svenskbyborna*, 75.
[57] DADO, f. 134, op. 1, spr. 8, arkk. 220-232; *Voenno-statisticheskoe obozrenie Rossiiskoi imperii*, t. 11, ch. 1, 93-94.
[58] Hedman, *Gammalsvenskby – the true story*.

hausendorf, Schlangendorf and Klosterdorf were grouped into a Swedish district with the centre in Gammalsvenskby.[59]

The Swedish-German relations can be characterized as ambivalent. The two groups were either peaceful neighbors, or irreconcilable rivals, sometimes even enemies. When relations were strained, the tension was usually due to disputes over land or religious differences. When faced with threats like epidemics, fires, nomad raids, or bad harvests, the Swedes and Germans united and helped each other.

Document 5: On bad harvest in the Swedish colony, 1899.

> According to the Swedish teacher of the colony, Christoffer Hoas, over half of the colonists are affected by real misery. The Germans in Tavriia province have already collected money for the villagers of Gammalsvenskby, who have received 250 Rubles from them.

Source: *"Från Ryssland," Nya Pressen*, 1900.01.29, no. 27.

However, when it came to electing the district mayor, the Swedes and the Germans were persistent opponents. The Swedish-German relations could be sketched within the following lines: conflict about the land, discord as to the religious question, but also economic and everyday interaction.

Generally, Swedish–German contacts can be described as interactive and important. The Germans and the Swedes shared several characteristics in material culture. They also had the Lutheran religion in common (except for the Catholic Germans from Klosterdorf). Accordingly, the cultural distance between them was comparatively small. In spite of the fact that the Swedes and the Germans had so much in common – much more than with other colonists in the region – marriages between Germans and Swedes were rare.[60] Having adopted the German style of dressing, the Swedes had to buy linen from the Germans after their spinning wheels had been destroyed in the fire of 1835 Some Germans enjoyed considerable prestige among the Swedes,

---

[59] *Antifeodalnaia borba volnykh shvedskikh krestian Estliandii 18–19 vv., sbornik dokumentov*, ed. Julius Madisson (Tallinn: Eesti raamat, 1978), 350.

[60] Iakov Shtakh, *Ocherki iz istorii i sovremennoi zhizni iuzhnorusskikh kolonistov* (Moskva: Tip. A. I. Mamontova, 1916), 112.

for example the military medical assistant Johann Glaubberg and the veterinary Fritz at Mühlhausendorf.[61]

The arrival of the Germans caused revolutionary changes in the farming methods of the Swedes. As mentioned above, the *ralo* used by the Swedes, was replaced with the German *bukker* plough with iron blades that increased agricultural productivity. Functionally a hybrid of the *ralo* and a multihued plough, the *bukker* was initially manufactured with three or four shares. This plough enabled a farmer, with no additional labour, to practically double the size of the area he cultivated. The price of these ploughs was not low enough to make them affordable for a poor farmer.[62] Among the Germans who influenced the farming metods of the Swedes one could in particular mention the Mennonite Johan Kornis who exercised great influence both as an agriculturist and educationalist,[63] and who in New Russia influenced different groups of the colonists including the Swedes.[64] The first Swedes that were sent for training to the Mennonite district of Molochna, were Anna Sergis and Cristian Tunis. Both of them became model farmers who passed on the new techniques they had learnt to others in the Swedish colony.[65]

As a result of cultural interaction with other ethnic groups, the Swedes had selectively acquired new cultural features. The colonist administration, the neighbors of the colonists, and the climatic and geographical milieu were decisive factors for their economic development and determined what fields they would specialize in. When they were hit by natural disasters, the different ethnic groups tended to cooperate more with each other than otherwise.

---

[61] Anton Karlgren, *Gammalsvenskby: land och folk, serie: svenska landsmål och svenskt folkliv* (Uppsala, 1929), 60–61.
[62] Leonard Friesen, "Bukkers, Plows and Lobogreikas: Peasant Acquistition of Agricultural Implements in Russia before 1900," *Russian Review*, t. 53, no. 3 (1994), 405.
[63] Mennonite Johan Kornis, the most skilled and successful farmer among the Germans and Mennonites in the region, was the head of Molochna agricultural association, the Association of forestation, sericulture and winemaking in Molochna Mennonite district in Tavriia province. He was also authorized to supervise schooling and agricultural education in Molochna Mennonite district.
[64] Ivan Zadereichuk, "Organizatsiino-pravova diialnist Johana Kornisa," *Forum prava*, no.1 (2008), 147–152.
[65] Karlgren, *Gammalsvenskby*, 76–77.

Preserving distinctiveness and becoming part of a whole

The natural resources of the region determined the shape of the Swedes' dwellings. The topography of Gammalsvenskby was a synthesis of the traditional dwellings of the Ukrainian villages and the Swedish settlements of north-western Estonia.[66] The clay-made houses dominated in the Ukrainian villages in the first half of the nineteenth century. Ordinary Ukrainian houses had no foundations, only an earth floor, and were made of clay and straw. Straw was the main roofing material.[67] The houses of the Swedish colonists were built in no particular order, along the main village road. This type of village structure was characteristic of the Swedish settlements in Estonia[68] and the Swedes seem to have brought it with them from there to the steppe.

In 1787–1788, an unknown Ukrainian master built a small wooden cruciform church in the centre of Gammalsvenskby. During the first five to ten years, the topography of the Swedish settlement was constantly changing and eventually it had shrunk in size. Due to the population decline, the areas south and north of the village center were abandoned. The inhabited areas consisted of two blocks called Taknegårda[69] and Nealinja. The fire in 1835 caused a radical reconstruction of Gammalsvenskby. The chaotic structure of the village was replaced by a geometrically organized one and the new Swedish houses were built along three main streets.[70]

Timber was used to a lesser extent because of its scarcity on the steppe, which also made it expensive. Clay, straw, vine, natural stone, seashell were the main building materials for the Swedish houses. The Swedes were well acquainted with stone as a building material since Dagö times. It was cheap and durable and could thus compensate for the lack of timber in the region.[71] Some of the Swedes built stone walls around their non-framed houses.[72] The exterior of the Swedish houses looked like typical Ukrainian buildings. However, the interior had its

---

[66] Gea Troska, "Poselenie pribrezhnykh shvedov," in *Skandinavskii sbornik*, no.21 (1976), 172–187; Kultura i pobut naselennia Ukrainy, ed. Vsevolod Naulko etc. (Kyiv: Lybid, 1991), 83–86.
[67] *Ocherki istorii nemtsev i mennonitov*, Bobyleva, 168.
[68] Troska, "Poselenie pribrezhnykh shvedov," 175.
[69] Literally meant the farms of the people from the Takne village.
[70] Lagus, "Utflygt till Dniepern," 549.
[71] *Samuil Khristianovich Contenius*, Eisfeld, 133; Lagus, "Utflygt till Dniepern," 549.
[72] *Samuil Khristianovich Contenius*, Eisfeld, 150–158; *Ukrainske narodoznavstvo*, ed. Stepana Pavliuka etc. (Lviv, 1994), 462–463.

special characteristics. The stove, the walls and the ceiling were whitewashed; the floor was made of clay, and in the winter covered with sand and in the summer with grass. Later, the floor in the houses of prosperous Swedes was made of wood.[73] The roof was not coated; the ceiling was crossed with thick whitewashed wooden beams. In front of the house, there was a hall and in the middle there was a kitchen, with several bedrooms attached to it. In contemporary sources it is said that the Swedish and German houses had a similar planning.[74]

Contemporary sources also say that the portraits of the Russian Tsar family appeared on the walls of the Swedish houses. When the colonists established contact with Sweden, portraits of the Swedish Royal family also became common. As the Swedish community was deeply religious, richly decorated pictures with Bible psalms, on the walls were typical of the Swedish houses. According to documented descriptions, in the right corner of the Swedish hall, there was a portrait of Martin Luther but, unlike the Orthodox religious tradition concerning pictures of the saints, there were no lights or candles in front of it.[75]

The food the Estonian Swedes ate in New Russia was mainly the same as that which they had eaten on Dagö but it was slightly adapted to the conditions of their new surroundings. Bread played an important role. The Swedish colonists preferred wheat bread, which was traditionally baked with yeast. More seldom, they made rye bread. As a rule, breakfast consisted of bread and butter and coffee mixed with chicory and vanilla. What was served for supper depended on the season: river fish and sour milk in the summer, noodle soup, meat with carrots and potatoes, and porridge in the winter. Swedish homemade sour cheese was very popular among the locals at the markets all over Kherson province.

Cross-influences between the Swedes and the Ukrainian and Russian peasants were common. Travellers and ethnographers noted that some traditional Slavic meals such as *kvas*[76] gained popularity among the Swedes. Moreover, besides coffee the Swedes enjoyed drinking tea, using

---

[73] Anton Karlgren, "Gammalsvenskby," in *Nordisk familjebok: Konversationslexikon och realencyklopedi*, vol. 9 (Stockholm: Nordisk familjeboks förlags aktiebolag, 1908), 705–708.
[74] Olga Chaika, "Usadba, dom i byt mennonitov v 19 veke," *Muzeinyi visnyk*, 2001: 1, 56–59; Chumachenko, "Shvedske poselennia na pivdni Ukrainy," 106–107.
[75] Utas, *Svenskbyborna*, 85.
[76] *Kvas* (Russian: квас, Ukrainian: квас) is a fermented beverage made from black or regular rye bread. It is classified as a non-alcoholic drink, as the alcohol content from fermentation is typically less than 1.2%.

a *samovar*.⁷⁷ The Swedes even used to cook *varenyky*,⁷⁸ a traditional Ukrainian meal, filling it with meat, mushrooms, fish, carrot, and rice.⁷⁹

During the first fifty years of steppe life, the design of the Swedes' clothing was a synthesis of originally Swedish elements of clothing and some northern Estonian features. After the fire of 1835, they had to give up their old-fashioned clothes. Their new clothes borrowed some elements from their German and Slavic neighbors. The Swedish winter clothes were, like those of Ukrainian and Russian peasants, made of fur and leather. The summer clothing was very simple, made of cotton and linen.⁸⁰ In the summer, the Swedes used shoes without heels. Men were only dressed in a shirt, trousers and a straw hat, women in linen clothing, slim skirt, and head-scarf.⁸¹

Thus, the material culture of the Swedish colonists reflected their background, as well influences from other ethnic groups in New Russia and the process of socio-cultural adaptation they were undergoing.

Religiosity is considered to have been the main element of premodern peasant identity. It was viewed as a pillar of stability, and therefore supported and promoted by the authorities. The Church had social control over its parishioners and influenced their everyday life.⁸²Absolute obedience to the Law of the Church, going to church every Sunday and observing religious holidays was the duty of all colonists in New Russia. A parishioner who neglected this duty was usually fined. Serious cases of neglect were punished more severely; in addition to paying a double fine, the delinquent would be sentenced to communal works, such as bridge repairing, tree planting, trench digging etc.⁸³

---

⁷⁷ Afanasiev-Chuzhbynskyi, *Podorozh u Pivdennu Rosi iu*, 261.
⁷⁸ Varenyky (Ukrainian: вареники) are similar to Polish pierogi, Russian pelmeni, and Italian ravioli.
⁷⁹ Karlgren, *Gammalsvenskby*, 46–47, 60.
⁸⁰ Karlgren, *Gammalsvenskby*, 48–49.
⁸¹ Aino Voolmaa, Melanie Kaarma, "Estonskii natsionalnyi kostium," *Iunyi khudozhnik*, no. 2 (1983), accessed March 22, 2009, http://dress-history.sageway.info/estonian-dress.html; DAOO, f. 6, op. 1, spr. 233, arkk. 12–13; Afanasiev-Chuzhbynskyi, *Podorozh u Pivdennu Rosiu*, 258.
⁸² Olga Litsenberger, "Problemy nravstvennosti v deiatelnosti Liuteranskoi i Katolicheskoi tserkvei," *Kliuchevyie problem istorii rossiiskikh nemtsev. Materialy X-I mezhdunarodnoi nauchnoi konferentsii. Moskva 18-21.11.2003* (Moskva: ZAO MSNK-press, 2004), 218.
⁸³ *Nemtsy v istorii Rossii*, Diesendorf, 116.

After the expiry of the grace period,[84] the colonists communities were expected to support their Lutheran or Catholic pastors and priests by themselves, and the government no longer paid their salaries.[85] The village headman was to make sure that every colonist aged sixteen to sixty paid his due three times a year (in January, May, and September).[86]

After departure of the first Gammalsvenskby priest Adolf Europeus, the German Lutheran priests from the nearby German colony of Jozefstal visited the Swedish village once a year. They stayed in the Swedish colony for a month to perform religious rites and to teach the Swedish children the basics of the Christian faith.[87] The Swedes were not satisfied with this occasional religious service; therefore in 1816 they complained to the caretaker Dalke that they did not have any priest at all. In November 1816, the Guardianship Office decided that a Catholic priest should visit Gammalsvenskby twice a year – in spring and in winter.[88]

In 1832 de jure recognition of its status as a denomination was granted to the Evangelical Lutheran Church in Russia. This meant that all Lutheran parishes in the entire Russian Empire were reorganized.[89] The Lutheran Swedes were incorporated into the St Petersburg Church district, but still their parish had been without the services of a priest long periods of time. The mere existence of the church organization did not mean it actually functioned in the empire's periphery.

The Swedish colonists in New Russia used the rune calendar, which signified to the contemporaries – the outsiders but also neighbors – the Swedes' distinctive origin, as well as original method of numbering years and measuring time.[90] Christmas, Midsummer (end of June) and St Martin's Day (11 November) were the most important holidays. Christmas was the main holiday of the year for the Swedish colonists, just as Easter was for the Ukrainian and Russian peasants. As a rule

---

[84] As a rule, the grace period, covered the first ten years after the migrants' resettlement to New Russia, was given by the Russian State in order to stimulate the colonists' economic development and speed their adaptation in new region.
[85] DAOO, f. 6, op. 1, spr. 777, arkk. 1–16.
[86] *Nemtsy v istorii Rossii*, Diesendorf, 117.
[87] DAOO, f. 6, op. 1, spr. 1672, arkk. 1–11; spr. 56, arkk. 10,34.
[88] DAOO, f. 6, op. 1, spr. 1025, arkk. 1–5; Olga Litsenberger, *Evangelichesko-liuteranskaia tserkov v Rossiiskoi imperii (XVI–XX vv.)* (Sankt-Peterburg: "Liuteranskoe kulturnoe nasledie," 2003), 136–137.
[89] Litsenberger, *Evangelichesko-liuteranskaia tserkov v Rossiiskoi imperii*, 82–84.
[90] Jörgen Hedman, Lars Åhlander, *Historien om Gammalsvenskby och svenskarna i Ukraina* (Stockholm: Dialogos, 2003), 13.

Midsummer and St Martin's Day, being Germanic holidays, were unknown to the Ukrainian and Russian locals.[91]

The school in Gammalsvenskby played a dominant role in teaching the young members of the community the Lutheran creed. They were taught and brought up under the pastor's strict control and were protected from interference by the government as long as it was possible. According to the Swedish Church Ordinance of 1686, the priests were to provide the parishioners with knowledge that would strengthen their faith. The Swedish colonist priest combined the functions of organist, teacher, and spiritual leader of the community. There was a close link between the school and the colonist community, which provided financial support to the school.[92] The compulsory training of all children of school age was not so strictly enforced within the Swedish community as among the Mennonite colonists, who controlled the fulfillment of this obligation consistently.[93] In the 1850s, only three Swedish farmers out of twenty-seven male grown-ups could write; the level of female literacy is unknown, as it is largely neglected in the sources.[94] However, most Swedish colonists, both men and women, could read and knew the basics of the Bible.

Beginning from the early nineteenth century, Swedish children aged from seven to fifteen (up to their confirmation) were taught at the teacher's house, where they studied German, the basics of Geography, handwriting, Bible history, Arithmetic, singing, and read the Scripture.[95] The school year usually lasted from 1 October until 1 May, sometimes from 1 November until 1 April, as the children had to work on the farms.[96]

Radical changes in imperial policy towards the non-Russian and non-Orthodox population of the empire, and the following campaign of Russification had a profound impact on all foreign colonists in New Russia.[97] In the 1860s the Trustees Committee officially introduced the Russian language into the colonist schools' curriculum as a compulsory

---

[91] Elena Shishkina-Fisher, *Nemetskie narodnye kalendarnye obriady, tantsy i pesni v Germanii i Rossii* (Moskva: "Mezhdunarodnyi soiuz nemetskoi kultury," 2002), 225-229, 307–309; Anton Karlgren, *Gammalsvenskby: land ock folk* (Stockholm: Kungl. Boktryckeriet, 1929), 62.
[92] DAOO, f. 6, op. 1, spr. 3717, ark. 44; spr. 4415, arkk. 17, 19; spr. 4450, arkk. 94, 97.
[93] *Ocherki istorii nemtsev i mennonitov*, Bobyleva, 145-147,149-150.
[94] DAOO, f. 6, op. 1, spr. 19678, ark. 24.
[95] DAOO, f. 6, op. 1, spr. 4415, ark. 17; spr. 4450, ark. 97.
[96] DAOO, f. 6, op. 1, spr. 4415, ark. 17; spr. 4450, ark. 97.
[97] James Urry, "Mennonites, Nationalism and the State in Imperial Russia," in *Journal of Mennonite Studies*, vol.12 (1994), 65–75.

subject. Henceforth Russian-German bilingualism was to be discouraged and suppressed, and instead Russian became the only language of administration in the colonies.[98] As they were the first foreign colonists in New Russia and were not German native speakers, the Swedes had, in order to facilitate communication with the colonial administration and their neighbors, started to learn Russian long before they were required to do so by the government.

The Swedish colonist community was a typical patriarchal peasant society with its characteristic forms of socialization and transmission of cultural roles, knowledge, experience, gender order, and the unquestioned authority of elders. The colonists' understanding of their identity was that which predominated in early modern society; it was based on religion, language and medieval privileges.[99] The status granted to them by Swedish law and the privileges they had enjoyed on Dagö, and the colonist status they had in New Russia helped them maintain their identity in both Estonia and Russia.

Eventually the Swedish ethnic identity, which had long remained based on religion, origin and language, was transformed into a new colonist identity based on their membership of a colony and their place of residence. The pastors who arrived from remote parts of the Russian Empire's Northwest (Adolf Europeus, Alexander Nordgren) were not only the carriers of the religious knowledge and background common to the Swedes, but also symbolically linked colonists with their former native island. Regarding the Swedes' self-identification, they did not initially identify themselves with Swedes from mainland Sweden, as had been suggested by Russian travelers, contemporaries and imperial officials from the middle of the nineteenth century.

Separation and inclusion, uniformity and diversity, which became permanent features of the Russian imperial policy, along with the missions of Finish and Swedish visitors to the village, promoted the creation of a particular "Gammalsvensk" tradition and culture. The tendency towards cultural conservatism and continuation of traditions intertwined with borrowing and adaptation of new cultural codes in the new milieu and emergence of a new "synthesized" tradition and dialect characteristic of Gammalsvenskby.

[98] *Ocherki istorii nemtsev i mennonitov*, Bobyleva, 151.
[99] Piotr Wawrzeniuk, "Tradition and Past: The Swedes of Alt-Schwedendorf 1782–1852," in *Voprosy germanskoi istorii*, ed. Svetlana Bobyleva (Dnipropetrovsk: Porogi, 2007), 12–19.

According to ethnographer Alexander Afanasiev-Chuzhbynskyi who visited the colony in the late 1850s, the inhabitants of the Swedish colony were noted for their law-obedience and respect for legal procedures, their honesty, diligence and loyalty to the state and other authorities.[100] Religious intolerance as well as conversions to other faiths were rare among them.[101] As a rule they endeavored to solve socio-economic and everyday problems by sending complaints, petitions and requests to the authorities of the state.[102] There was no unrest or agitation in Gammalsvenskby, and crimes were rare.[103] The low delinquency among the relatively few Swedes contrasted to nearby numerous German colonists', who were occasionally condemned for various misdemeanors, sexual crimes, appropriation of property and disobedience towards authorities.[104] The Swedish colonists were regarded as loyal subjects of the Russian Tsar and were not as opposed to Russification and other crucial changes in official policy towards the colonists as the Germans and Mennonites in the region.

Conclusions

As a result of acculturation, and in exchange for privileges connected to the colonist status, the Baltic islanders became loyal colonists and empire-builders. Empire-builders came in many forms – settlers, missionaries, officials, prisoners, as well as governor-generals and generals. The Swedish colonists contributed to the imperial project of transformation and reinventing of the steppe by pursuing different economic activities promoted by the government. To abstain from taking part in them was hardly possible, no matter what the Swedes thought about the prospects of the experiments.

---

[100] DAOO, f. 6, op. 1, spr. 349, arkk. 2,24; DADO, f. 134, op. 1, spr. 512, ark. 22; Afanasiev-Chuzhbynskyi, *Podorozh u Pivdennu Rosiiu*, 257-261.
[101] Utas, *Svenskbyborna*, 83.
[102] *Antifeodalnaia borba volnykh shvedskikh krestian*, Madisson, 31–32, 39–40,52–53,129,131–133, 332–333; DAOO, f. 6, op. 1, spr. 56, ark. 10; spr. 128, ark. 9; spr. 1025, arkk. 1–3.
[103] Olga Konovalova, "Kolonisty Iuga Rossii v konflikte s zakonom (1800-1818)," in *Voprosy germanskoi istorii*, ed. Svetlana Bobyleva (Dnipropetrovsk: Porogi, 2007), 98-105; DAOO, f. 6, op. 1, spr. 1706, arkk. 10,110; spr. 889, arkk. 1-3; spr. 1131, arkk. 1-11; spr. 4279, arkk. 3-8.
[104] DAOO, f. 6, op. 1, spr. 608, arkk. 1-36; spr. 613, arkk. 1-40; spr. 767, arkk. 1-11; spr. 617, arkk. 1-17; spr. 1093, arkk. 1-29; spr. 767, arkk. 1-11; spr. 892, arkk. 1-8; spr. 1099, arkk. 1-22; spr. 1181, arkk. 1-7.

As Willard Sunderland emphasizes, by the dawn of the twentieth century, the steppe had been so profoundly transformed by Russian imperialism that it was difficult for contemporaries to determine whether it constituted a borderland, a colony, or Russia itself. It seemed hard to believe that the plains could ever have belonged to anyone else except Russia.[105]

Along with transforming the steppe, the Swedish community itself experienced a number of radical transformations: physical (migration and then residence in new geographical and social milieu); juridical (the status changes: the loss of medieval privileges and obtaining of the colonist status that guaranteed the rights and privileges in Russia, required some obligations); economical (the changes in economic specialization of the Swedes, managing certain economic activities unknown before). The indigenous population, other foreign colonists, and the authorities were the key actors that influenced and predetermined the specifics and the extent of the Swedes' integration and acculturation in southern Russia. Apart from preserving some cultural elements as their traditional food and their rune calendar, the Swedish colonists borrowed the trends of garment, furnishings from their German and Slavic neighbors that proved the intercultural dialogue. Unlike such non-numerous groups as Serbs, Montenegrins, Hungarians, Italians, French speaking Swiss, the inhabitants of Gammalsvenskby managed to avoid assimilation in the nineteenth century.

---

[105] Sunderland, *Taming the Wild Field*, 89, 223, 228.

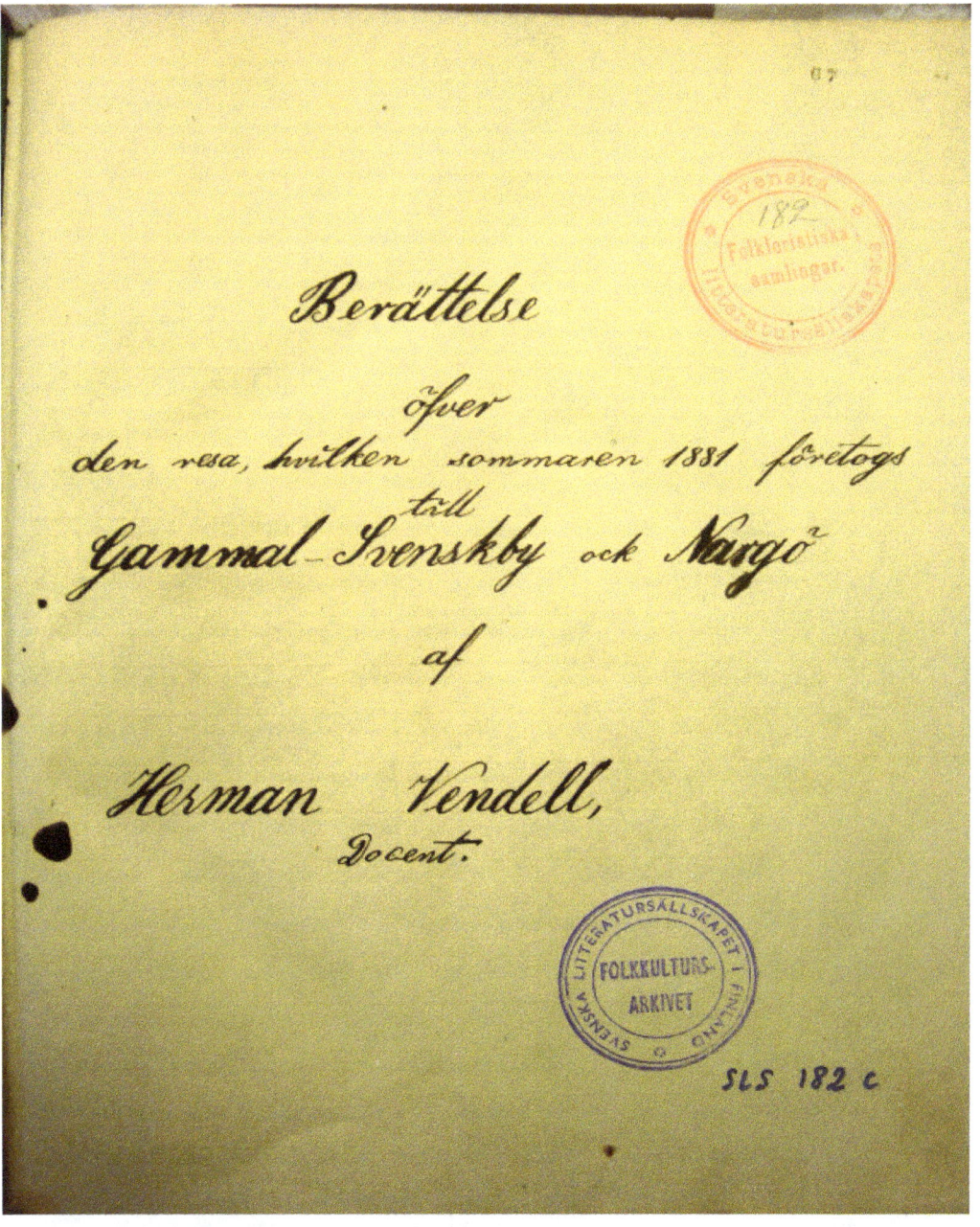

Illustration 1: The first page of Herman Vendell's travel account from his fieldtrip in 1881 to Gammal-svenskby and Nargö, an island in the Tallinn Bay. After returning to Finland, he published several articles influential in shaping of the public imagination about the village in Finland and Sweden. SLS FS, SLS 182c.

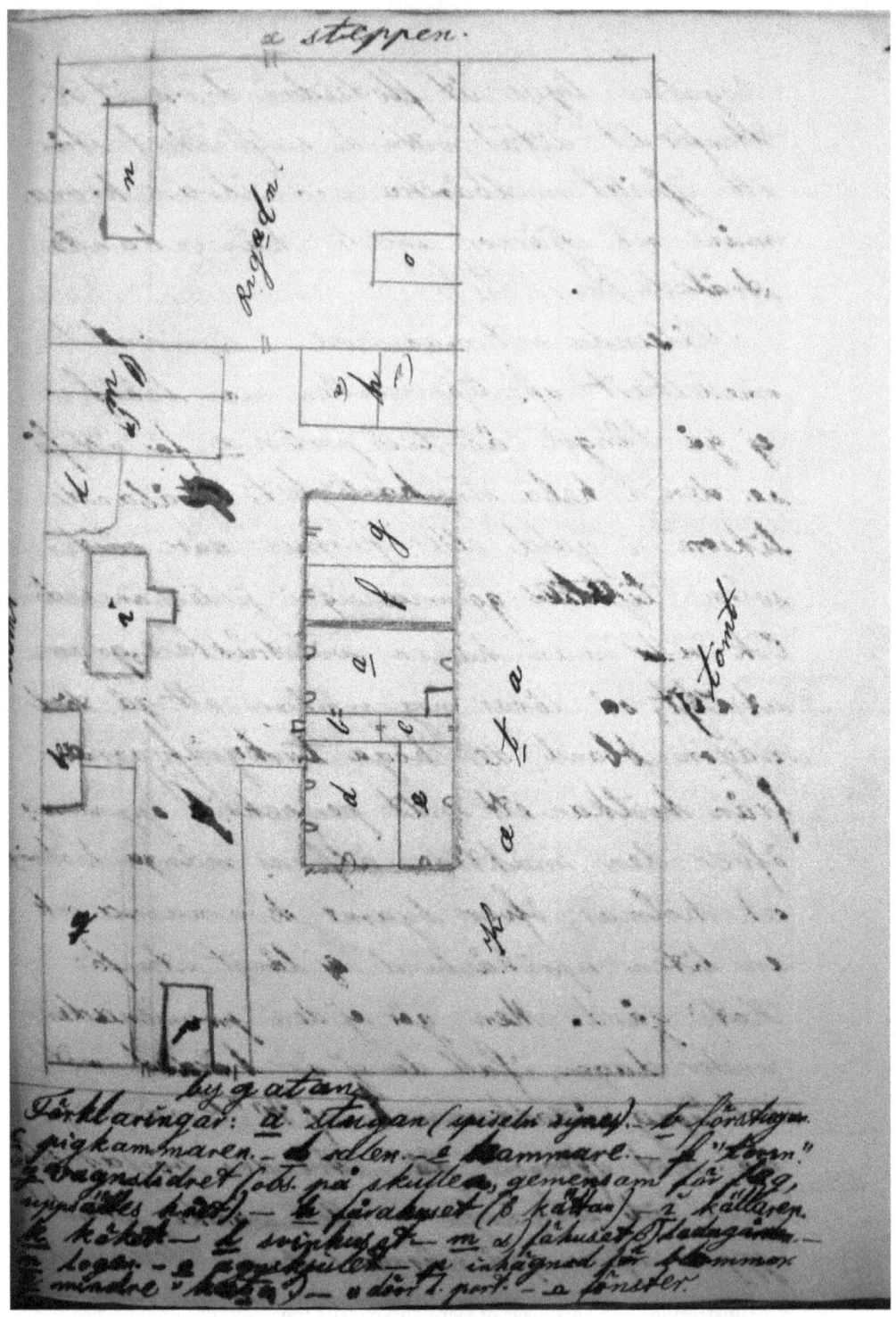

Illustration 2: Beyond pure linguistics. Although a linguist himself, Vendell's wide field of interest turned him into a scientific omnivore. Here is a sketch of the farmstead where Vendell stayed during his work in Gammalsvenskby. SLS FS, SLS 182c.

The Making of Gammalsvenskby 1881–1914
– identity, myth and imagination

PIOTR WAWRZENIUK

The title of this chapter points at a long process during which the image of Gammalsvenskby was "created," so to say, in the interaction between the villagers, their neighbors, the authorities, and the Finnish and Swedish visitors and press. By the advent of the First World War, the image of the village in the accounts of visitors and press was an amalgamation of various cultural elements and processes. The cultural legacy with roots in the pre-migration times was very much present, somewhat altered by developments since the migrants from Dagö settled there in 1782 and the specific geographical, cultural, and judicial milieu of the colonists in the South of the Russian Empire. In addition, the image of the village was strongly influenced by contact between the villagers and Swedish speaking visitors from Finland and Sweden. These encounters became frequent only from the 1880s, after word about the village was spread in Swedophone newspapers in Sweden, Finland and the US. The village faced the diverse visions of what it meant to be a Swede according to the ideas of ethnic nationalism imported from Finland and Sweden.

In this chapter the village is seen as a cultural construct, created and kept alive within a network of social relations. Gammalsvenskby existed in the sphere of imagination, rather than as merely a geographic locality within the administrative limits of the Swedish colonist district.[1] The above-mentioned point allows for following the process of imagining and describing of Gammalsvenskby and its surroundings. Cultural delimitations are a product of social relations, a creation of groups and individuals.[2] This

---

[1] Lars-Olov Sjöström, *Modernitet i det traditionella – Kulturbyggen och gränser inom ett nordsvenskt område* (Umeå: H:ström Text & Kultur, 2007), 30.
[2] Sjöström, *Modernitet*, 31.

perspective proves particularly fruitful when studying the construction of the village in the accounts of visitors and newspapers.

This chapter will mainly deal with how the image of the village was shaped and kept alive from the time when durable contacts were established between Gammalsvenskby and various circles in Finland and Sweden in 1881 up to the outbreak of the First World War in 1914. However, first it is necessary to see what elements were decisive for the identity formation of the villagers before regular contacts with Sweden and Finland started. Then the author will then proceed with a presentation of the ideas that influenced the visitors and contributed to shaping the image of the village among in the public in Finland and Sweden. Two individuals whose views on Gammalsvenskby can be seen as somewhat symbolic – Herman Vendell and Emma Skarstedt – have been chosen for this purpose. Their accounts were basically in binary opposition to each other when the village was discussed; Vendell was an idealist while Skarstedt was a weary realist. Finally, the text will follow the creation of the myth of the village as a fortress of patriotic Swedishness, and its population as the lost Swedish tribe.

This basically romantic and nationalistic view of the villagers as timeless vessels of Swedish and Germanic virtues prevailed until the late 1920s, and exercised great influence when – in combination with the deterioration of the living conditions of the villagers under Soviet rule – a belief grew in Sweden that the villagers should be brought back into the bosom of the Swedish nation. Once in Sweden many of the former villagers were not content with what Sweden was prepared to offer. Horrified Swedish officials discovered that the former Gammalsvenskby dwellers lacked many qualities expected from a modern Swede and that – perhaps – the racial purity of the resettled group might be in doubt.[3]

When differences matter

When studying the formation of identity and acculturation (understood as cautious and selective adaptation to, but not assimilation into, the dominant society) of the villagers, it is important to keep in mind that ethnicity becomes relevant in a social situation where cultural differences assume significance; there must exist at least one group that is regarded as different from the

---

[3] Anna Wedin, "Gammalsvenskbybornas emigration till Sverige 1929. En studie i svenskhet och etniskt ursprung," Unpublished Bachelor Thesis in history supervised by Andrej Kotljarchuk (Södertörn University, 2007).

others.⁴ An ethnic group will retain its separateness only as long as its members hold on to specific traditions, customs or other characteristics that can be seen as symbols of their separateness, such as language, a kinship system, an old religion, or a certain way of life. Usually, in the circumstances viewed as dangerous by a group, dramatic experiences activate one or several of such symbols. Anthropologist Thomas Hylland Eriksen identifies migration, demographic changes, and integration or incorporation into a wider political system as such experiences.⁵ The villagers and their migrating ancestors went through virtually all of this. Their move from Dagö and resettlement in Ukraine and the extreme mortality levels during the migration and the initial years on the steppe can be mentioned as examples. They brought with them a strong sense of separateness from Dagö, then developed and nurtured in the new conditions of the colonist life.

The strong group coherence and the principle of exclusiveness that for a long time guided the villagers in their relations with outsiders, is reminiscent of the behavior covered by the sociological term sect. Such a group views itself as the sole bearer of truth. The members are in a small minority in society, but are expected to live according to a strict set of teachings. There is often a measure of suspicion between the sect and the surrounding society. While the sect views itself as unique and the outside society as potentially dangerous and in a state of moral and religious decay, others frequently regard the sect as dissenting and problematic.⁶ In the following paragraphs several examples will be given of the exclusivist approach the villagers took, but also of the negative view their closest neighbors, the German settlers, had of them.

The persistence of the past
– Gammalsvenskby and its early modern features

The inhabitants of Gammalsvenskby managed to preserve their Swedish identity because the village was a peasant society which, until the mid-nineteenth century, retained many features that were typical of the early modern era. This does not mean the village was an entirely static society. However, there was a deep attachment to old customs and the ways of the ancestors. In order to identify these features, reports by people who visited

---

⁴ Thomas Hylland Eriksen, *Etnicitet och nationalism* (Nora: Nya Doxa, 1998), 29, 45, 47.
⁵ Eriksen, *Etnicitet*, 89–90; citation, 89.
⁶ Inger Furuseth, Pål Repstad, *Religionssociologi – en introduktion* (Malmö: Liber, 2008), 184-185.

the village have been used.⁷ The group coherence and solidarity between the villagers were kept alive by their common ancestry, their language and religion, and their collective memory of their special status as free peasants on Dagö.

Religion was an important component of a pre-modern peasant's identity. A large number of books among those available to the villagers of Gammalsvenskby, religious books printed in Stockholm and Reval are mentioned along with schoolbooks from Åbo. The schoolteacher used these books in accordance with the "Old Swedish Church Law" (apparently the Church Ordinance of 1686, as no other Church Ordinance was promulgated before Dagö passed from Swedish to Russian control in 1710).⁸ The use of the old versions of the Hymn Book and the Bible by the villagers constantly turned their attention not only towards God and prayer, but also towards their past as Swedish subjects. In this way links to the past were maintained, and contributed considerably to preservation of the Swedish identity.

From early on there were also other features that preserved the common group identity of the Swedes. The village in which they lived was eventually named Staroshvedskaia, literally "Old-Swedish Village." Together with the German villages of Mühlhausendorf, Schlangendorf and Klosterdorf it later constituted the "Old-Swedish" district. The authorities also pursued a deliberate policy of differentiating between the various ethnic groups among the settlers. In a list of people who inhabited the village in August 1808, the Swedes who migrated from Dagö in 1781 are separated from people from Poland and Danzig, who arrived later. Even the Swedish prisoners of war who settled in the village in 1790 were registered in separate tables when the population and its property were counted.⁹ When the villagers were given last names in 1860s, many referred to the names of farms, other place names, and patronyms from Dagö. This shows that memories from the island were still alive, and the old distinctions still mattered in 1860s.

---

⁷ Reports written by August Nymann (1836), Wilhelm Lagus (1852), A. Afanasiev-Chuzhbynskyi (1863), Herman Vendell (1881-1882), Anton Karlgren (1906), Herman Neander (1912) are used. All of the reporters but Nymann, who sent a servant, visited the village in person. The accounts of the stays in the village were published in newspapers, journals and books. Apart from the reports, a letter written by three villagers to Haapsalu school inspector Carl Russwurm in 1849 (published 1850) is used. As to archival sources, materials deposited at DADO, DAKhO are used along with material from RGIA.

⁸ Piotr Wawrzeniuk, "Tradition and the Past: The Swedes of Alt-Schwedendorf 1782–1852," in *Voprosy germanskoi istorii*, ed. Svetlana Bobyleva (Dnipropetrovsk: Porogi, 2007), 12–19.

⁹DADO, f.134, op.1, spr. 193.

In the preceding pages, about the early modern features of the villagers, one finds several characteristics reminiscent of the term sect: a tendency to keep a distance to outsiders who were not prepared to adapt to the culture of the villagers; pressure on the members of the community not to leave the village for any considerable period of time (and thus no longer under the influence of the village collective). We also find that there were spiritual leaders who ensured the old customs lived on in an almost unadulterated version. At the same time, there were many elderly people who maintained the continuity between the old and the new, and whose words were respected. Add to that a sense of common ancestry (history, language, religion), strengthened by the trauma of migration, and the long-term survival of group solidarity and the coherence of the group becomes understandable.

Polish anthropologist Ludwik Stomma has argued that the peasantry under Romanov and Habsburg rule in the nineteenth century was a spatially, socially and mentally isolated group. The mental isolation made the peasant society resistant to adaptation to impulses from the outside world. In addition to that, few peasants travelled beyond their native region or mixed with other social groups, thus adding spatial and social isolation to the mental one. It was a culture that frequently looked to the past for guidance and referred to primeval state in a remote past. A natural order of things in ancient times, an essence of things, are standard components of what the past may have to offer in form of guidance.[10]

Four reports about the village between 1836 and 1912 (Nymann, Lagus, Vendell, and Neander) claim that the villagers seldom married outsiders. Marriages to Germans or other outsiders were very uncommon.[11] Herman Neander who visited the village in the early twentieth century claimed that many among the villagers were genetically closely related, as there were 140 families, but only 22 family names.[12] Herman Vendell explained the beauty of the village women with the fact that marriages with outsiders were *"not practiced"* (emphasis added); this allowed the villagers to retain their

---

[10] Ludwik Stomma, *Antropologia kultury wsi polskiej XIX w.* (Warszawa: Instytut Wydaw. Pax, 1986), 65–77, 143, 146.
[11] Wilhelm Lagus, "Utflygt till Dniepern i April 1852," *Finlands Allmänna Tidning*, no.132 (1852), 549.
[12] Herman Neander, *Gammal-Svenskby* (Stockholm: Hugo Gebers förlag, 1912), 17. In fact, by the time Neander wrote his book, the situation was already changing. The Parish Register suggests that 9 of 23 marriages (almost 40 per cent) in Alt-Schwedendorf in the years 1899 and 1903–1905 were mixed marriages. One can hardly treat this number as insignificant; DAKhO, f. 232, op.1, spr.1, arkk. 34, 90, 133, 182.

Swedish physiognomy.[13] Karlgren wrote about their reluctance "to bring alien elements into the village;" if such marriages were at all contracted, they involved a Swede and a German, but never a person of Slavic origin.[14]

In a letter written in 1849 to school inspector Carl Russwurm, Haapsalu, three representatives of the villagers claimed there were 52 families of "pure Swedes" (*rena swänskar*) before providing the exact numbers of men, women and children in these families.[15] They did not write "villagers" or "locals," which would have been more inclusive, they wrote "pure Swedes". Wilhelm Lagus reported that few Swedes ever left the village for seasonal work, as this was unpopular with the village collective. At the same time, he noted that the relations between villagers were "thoroughly patriarchal," as "everything they [the villagers] know has its root in their [the elders'] experience."[16]

Lagus' observations were later confirmed by ethnographer Alexander Afanasiev-Chuzhbynskyi, who after several visits to the village in the early 1860s described the relations between the Swedes as "kindly patriarchal."[17] In the early twentieth century, a Swedish visitor to the village, Anton Karlgren, also characterized relations between the villagers as "thoroughly patriarchal," adding that the young had great respect for the elders.[18] According to another Swedish visitor, contemporary with Karlgren, the villagers "treated each other almost as members of the same family."[19]

The letter from 1849 quoted above from the villagers also suggests that customs from Dagö remained largely intact, with the exception of the language used at weddings and baptisms, a change that is readily explained by the fact that these spiritual services were provided by German pastors.

Some individuals played a leading role in the preservation of traditions and customs. Mats Magnusson Kotz (1756–1839), bell-ringer and parish schoolteacher, was an important mediator between the present and the past.

---

[13] SLS FS, SLS 182c, "Berättelse öfver den resa, hvilken sommaren 1881 företogs till Gammal-Svenskby ock Nargö af Herman Vendell, Docent" (Docent Herman Vendell's Account of His Journey to Gammalsvenskby and Nargö in the Summer of 1881), 94.
[14] Anton Karlgren, *Gammalsvenskby: land och folk, serie: svenska landsmål och svenskt folkliv* (Uppsala, 1929), 43
[15] Carl Russwurm, "Om svensk koloni wid Dniepern," *Helsingfors Tidningar*, no. 31(1850), 404.
[16] Lagus, "Utflygt till Dniepern," 549.
[17] Anatolii Afanasiev-Chuzhbynskyi, *Podorozh u Pivdennu Rosiiu* (Dnipropetrovsk: Sich, 2005), 253–254.
[18] Jörgen Hedman, Lars Åhlander, *Historien om Gammalsvenskby och svenskarna i Ukraina* (Kristianstad: Dialogos, 2003), 121.
[19] Neander, *Gammal-Svenskby*, 17.

He was mentioned in the first report about the village in 1836 as the villagers' tutor in religion, and was mentioned again in the letter in 1849.[20] In fact, his function seems to have been similar to that of the anthropological notion of a guru. A guru adds "personal charisma to book-learning, in a combination of oral and literate modes of communication." In societies where literacy is limited, the art of narration flourishes.[21] Kotz seems to have been the main interpreter and mediator of knowledge linked to Dagö and the Lutheran religion in its seventeenth century version. Kotz performed this function of a "guru," a charismatic authority based on custom and personal authority, for over three decades.[22] After Mats Magnusson Kotz's death in 1839, his son Kristian Matsson Kotz took over this function, and was in his turn succeeded by his son Henrik Kristiansson Kotz in 1856.[23]

Kristian Matsson Kotz was one of three men who could read and understand Carl Russwurm's letter written in Swedish to the village and answer it in 1849. Apparently, literacy otherwise hardly extended beyond singing from the Hymn Book and reading the required parts of the Bible. In fact, only the three men who wrote the letter to Carl Russwurm in 1849 seem to have been fully literate (i.e., able both to read and to write) in Swedish; actually, in their letter they say they have joined forces in order to be able to write the text.[24]

The songs, riddles and proverbs of old Dagö times were preserved at least up to the First World War. They were reported to be disappearing from daily use, but had been recorded for future generations.[25] It seems likely that the oldest inhabitants of the village, who lived three or four decades into the nineteenth century, played a significant role in the transmission of customs to the younger generations. There were several elderly people in 1830s and 1840s who were adults or in their late teens at the time of the migration from Dagö: Mats Nilsson Buskas (1761–1836),

---

[20] Wawrzeniuk, "Tradition and the Past," 14–15.
[21] Jack Goody, "Introduction," in *Literacy in Traditional Societies*, ed. Jack Goody (Cambridge: Cambrigde University Press, 1968), 13.
[22] According to Max Weber, traditional authority is based on custom and presupposes limited reflection over alternative development; see Furuseth, Repstad, *Religionssociologi*, 195.
[23] Hedman, Åhlander, *Historien om Gammalsvenskbyn*,
[24] Carl Russwurm, "Om svensk koloni wid Dniepern," *Helsingfors Tidningar*, no. 31 (1850), 405.
[25] Neander, *Gammal-Svenskby*, 14; Sigfrid Hoas, *Banditer i byn. Min barndoms äventyr i Gammal-Svenskby* (Stockholm: Ev. fosterlandsstiftelsen, 1959), 12–20, Karlgren, *Gammalsvenskby*, 62.

Mickel Greisson Albers (1765–1844) and two women, Maria Matsdotter Mutas (born 1761) and Margareta Larsdotter Larsas (born 1767) both of whom lived well into 1830s. In fact, fifty out of 220 villagers in the 1830s were born in the eighteenth century. While the Swedish contemporary writers Jörgen Hedman and Lars Åhlander view it as a sign of the Dagö culture fading away, the number rather suggests that there was a large group of people in the village who had either personal experience or memories from the island, or had been told about life there by their parents.[26]

At the end of the nineteenth and the beginning of the twentieth century, people who were passing away were grandchildren of the colonists of 1782, and had probably encountered several elders from Dagö and the first generation of villagers born in Gammalsvenskby. Fourteen of those who died between 1905 and 1913 were born between 1816 and 1839. Two of them were born in the 1810s, two in 1820s and ten in the 1830s.[27] During the most labor intensive farming season, the adults were permanently on fields far away, leaving the running of the households "to the elderly and the children," Lagus reported.[28] This opened for socialization where material and oral culture could be transmitted to the younger generations.

The Swedish-Estonian historian Alexander Loit has studied the widespread favorable sentiments towards the Swedish Crown among the peasantry of Estonia and Livonia under Russian rule that was reported by ethnographers in the first half of the nineteenth century. The economic pressure from the landlords increased after the Russian take-over and in the collective memory of peasants the Swedish period is referred to as "the good old Swedish times." This somewhat idyllic view of the past mirrored the fact that serfdom was abolished during the rule of Charles XI, and a model of behavior developed where the peasants turned to their king for protection against their mainly Baltic German lords. The peasantry in Swedish Livonia was given the same rights and obligations as other peasants in the Swedish domains.[29] Needless to say, this interpretation of the past was even stronger among the Swedish peasants of Estonia and Livonia. They remembered being free men enjoying their rights and privileges (frequently codified in and

---

[26] Hedman, Åhlander, *Historien om Gammalsvenskyby*, 65.
[27] DAKhO, f. 323, op. 1, spr. 1, arkk.135-288; f. 323, op. 1, spr. 2, arkk. 36–299; f. 323, op.1, spr. 3, ark. 34.
[28] Lagus, "Utflygt till Dniepern," 545.
[29] Alexander Loit, „Die ‚alte gute Schwedenzeit' und ihre historische Bedeutung für das Baltikum," in (eds.) Carsten Goehrke; Jürgen von Ungern-Sternberg, *Die baltischen Staaten im Schnittpunkt der Entwicklungen: Vergangenheit und Gegenwart* (Basel: Schwabe, 2002), 76–88.

confirmed by letters from Swedish monarchs) that long preceded the brief emancipation of the peasants of Swedish Livonia. After the Russian take-over, the Swedish peasants referred to their rights as free men when faced with attempts by feudal lords to enserf them. At the end of the eighteenth and in the first half of the nineteenth century, runaways from islands and villages inhabited by Swedes sought refuge in Sweden from Russian military service and the exploitation at the hands of Baltic German lords.[30]

Thus, the villagers of Gammalsvenskby preserved their old customs and language thanks to the continuity in the spiritual leadership in the village, and the chariness of rapid change characteristic of peasant societies. Custom, religion and the historical memory continued to matter in the new surroundings. In fact, their importance even increased due to the vicissitudes of colonist life. The almost permanent crises in the village stimulated the preservation of the Swedish identity of the villagers and their group solidarity. The work of the three subsequent bell ringers and parish schoolteachers was carried out father, son, and a grandson, from 1782 and into 1860s. The overlapping of generations of people who remembered Dagö and the hardships of the first colonist decades, and people who were passing away in the beginning of the twentieth century, must also have stimulated the passing of the group's customs and beliefs to younger generations. The Swedish identity of the former islanders was also preserved by their attachment to a particular form of Lutheranism, the archaic Swedish language of the sacred texts they carried with them to southern Russia and collective memory that encompassed the rights and privileges as free yeomen under the rule of the Teutonic Order and Sweden.

Modernity and the village: nationalism and the social question

Gammalsvenskby was a comparatively isolated village. Outside it however, were currents that eventually influenced developments in the village. Generally, these processes can be viewed as challenges posed by modernity and the ways in which different groups handled them. In the case of the visitors to Gammalsvenskby, and the Swedish and Finnish media's descriptions of the village, growing cultural differentiation can be singled out as the most important of these challenges. A general tendency during the nineteenth century was a gradual diminishing of values that were shared by large groups in society, and the emergence of a multitude of different values

[30] Viktor Aman, *En bok om Estlands svenskar IV. Kulturhistorisk översikt* (Stockholm: Utg.,1992), 14–25.

and new ways of communicating them in politics, science and economy. The consolidation of the nation state and the rise of the so-called social movement, with its plethora of civic organizations, were two features of this process that were important for Gammalsvenskby.[31] The organizations linked to the social movement were often created as a reaction to rapid and deep societal changes. Their ambition was to change society, and people's ways of thinking and living, by organizing people for common action.[32] The growing organizational diversity was also mirrored by women's organizations, although there was a separate public sphere for women in the second half of the nineteenth century. In the beginning of the twentieth century, the restrictions on women's participation in public affairs decreased steadily.[33] It would be impossible to understand the creation of the image of Gammalsvenskby without taking into account the societal currents and political and cultural development in Finland and Sweden. Therefore, an outline of the relevant processes is presented below.

During most of the nineteenth century, Swedish nationalism was liberal. However, by the end of the century, the ruling dynasty had developed an official, conservative nationalism. At the end of the nineteenth and beginning of the twentieth century, there were numerous patriotic ceremonies, many museums were built and numerous monuments erected to commemorate the nation's great men, heroic achievements and culture.[34] In historiography, the national-romantic narrative focused on the people, and the era when Sweden was a great power. The narrative also stressed what its adherents viewed as a long tradition of freedom, with a free yeomanry, and the alliance between the King and the people as the bedrock of the realm.

The position of the Swedish peasantry, which was unique in the early modern period, was interpreted in terms of a millennium long era of liberty with roots in the times of the Germanic tribes.[35]

---

[31] Francis Sejersted, *Socialdemokratins tidsålder. Sverige och Norge under 1900-talet* (Stockholm: Nya Doxa, 2005), 8–11.

[32] Martin Stolare, *Kultur och natur. Moderniseringskritiska rörelser i Sverige 1900–1920* (Göteborg: Historiska institutionen, Univ., 2003), 13.

[33] Inger Hammar, *Emancipation och religion: den svenska kvinnorörelsens pionjärer i debatt om kvinnans kallelse ca 1860–1900* (Stockholm: Carlsson, 1999), 11; Lovisa af Petersens, *Formering för offentlighet. Kvinnokonferenser och Svenska Kvinnornas Nationalförbund kring sekelskiftet 1900* (Stockholm: Acta Universitatis Stockholmiensis, 2006), 28–29.

[34] Billy Ehn, Jonas Frykman, Orvar Löfgren, *Försvenskningen av Sverige: det nationellas förvandlingar* (Stockholm: Natur och kultur, 1993), 24–25, 43–47.

[35] Patrik Hall, *Den svenskaste historien: nationalism i Sverige under sex sekler* (Stockholm: Carlsson, 2000), 197; Sejersted, *Socialdemokratins tidsålder*, 15; Torbjörn Nilsson,

In Finland, Finnish nationalism was locked in fierce competition with the nationalism and aspirations of the Swedophone population (about 300,000 people in the 1880s) until the end of the nineteenth century. Several intellectuals among the Swedish-speaking Finns (the term "Finno-Swedish" – *finlandssvensk* – was not widely in use before the First World War) opposed the Finnish nationalism that promoted the Finnish language and Finnish culture as national, rather than the Swedish language that dominated in the administration at least up to 1866, when Finnish was introduced as a second official language. In the 1860s, the *Fennomaner*, as the Finnish activists were called in Swedish, were a relatively small group of Swedophone intellectuals who regarded the Swedish political and cultural domination of Finland as unjust. This energetic movement engaged in politics, achieving a majority among the peasant and priest estates in the Finnish Diet, 1877–1878, thereby alarming intellectuals who sympathized with the old order of things. The Swedish activists viewed the advance of the *Fennomaner* in the political and educational sphere as a threat to the very existence of the Swedish-Germanic culture (as opposed to the Finnish and Finno-Ugric one).

The conflict between *Fennomaner* and *Svekomaner* (as the adherents of strong position of Swedish culture and language were called) accelerated during the 1870s and 1880s. While the *Fennomaner* viewed Swedish culture as an obsolete remnant of an unjust order, several among the *Svekomaner* (sing.: *Svekoman*) thought that the Germanic (Swedish) race was superior to Asiatic peoples (according to the *Fennomaner*, the roots of the Finnish people were to be found in Ural Mountains and Siberia). Consequently, among the pioneers of the *Svekoman* movement in Helsinki, ancient Nordic culture (viewed as genuinely Germanic) was in high esteem. However, the conflict between the two groups was set aside as the Russification campaign launched from St Petersburg intensified towards the end the century.[36]

The abovementioned process was formative for Herman Vendell, a Swedophone Finnish linguist who visited Gammalsvenskby in 1881, and subsequently published influential accounts about the village. In a letter

---

Mellan arv och utopi: moderata vägval under 100 år, 1904-2004 (Stockholm: Santérus, 2004), 79–80.

[36] Ilkka Liikanen, *Fennomania ja kansa: joukkojärjestäytymisen läpimurto ja Suomalaisen puolueen synty* (Helsinki: Suomen historiallinen seura, 1995), 349–351, 357–358; Eino Jutikkala, Kauko Pirinen, *Finlands historia* (Stockholm: Natur och kultur, 1982 [1973]), 122, 129; Bo Lönnqvist, "Drakskepp och runslingor," in *Gränsfolkets barn: finlandssvensk marginalitet och självhävdelse i kulturanalytiskt perspektiv*, (eds) Anna-Maria Åström, Bo Lönnqvist, Yrsa Lindqvist, (Helsingfors: Svenska litteratursällsk. i Finland, 2001), 236.

Vendell wrote as a young man in 1876 to a Swedish relative he stressed that the culture of the Swedophones in Finland rested upon "folk songs and traditions, dialects and customs."[37] During his student years, Vendell collected language samples and other data about Swedophone inhabitants of Finland. In 1874, Vendell, and the leading *Svekoman* figure Axel Olof Freudenthal (later the first professor of Nordic languages at the Alexander University in Helsinki) and several others founded *Svenska landsmålsföreningen* (The Swedish Dialects Society).[38] Its main goal was the preservation of the Swedish language and culture, which "like everything Swedish" seemed to be doomed to drown "in the flood of advancing Finnish national and language ambitions," as Vendell put it when looking back in 1880s. The collection of dialects and other data was supposed to end what was perceived as the *Fennoman* denigration of Swedish culture in Finland.[39] *Svenska landsmålsföreningen* provided the funding for Vendell's journey to Gammalsvenskby and the Swedophone enclave of Nargö in Estonia in 1881. In 1885, the newly founded *Svenska litteratursällskapet i Finland, Folkkultursarkivet och språkarkivet* (The Swedish Literature Society in Finland, Archives of folklore and language) in Finland laid down detailed rules on the methods to be used and how to keep a diary while collecting dialect samples and artefacts of ethnological interest.[40] Vendell made considerable contributions to the collection of Swedish dialects in the Russian provinces of Estonia and Livonia, later also in Finland. His magnum opus, *Ordbok öfver de östsvenska dialekterna* (Dictonary of East-Swedish Dialects), was published shortly before his death in 1907.

The so-called social question in Sweden had strong moralistic connotations. The lower classes were frequently described as hopelessly poor, dirty, unhealthy, immoral, and leaning towards drunkenness. The tone in the bourgeois press was patronizing. As poverty was mainly considered to be due to the individual, education and moral elevation were seen as the remedy. A large number of voluntary organizations, whose tasks ranged from philanthropy and education to advocating temperance, were founded

---

[37] SLS HLA, SLSA 325, Herman Vendell to Henning Vendell, Ekenäs (Finland), 20 June 1876.
[38] Ulrika Wolf-Knuts, "Folkdikten och dess upptecknare," in *Finlands svenska litteraturhistoria* (Helsingfors & Stockholm: Svenska litteratursällsk. i Finland, 1999), 401.
[39] Herman Vendell, "Svenska landsmålsföreningen i Helsingfors 1874–1881," *De Svenska Landsmålsföreningarna i Uppsala, Helsingfors och Lund 1872–1881*, one of booklets of *Nyare Bidrag Om De Svenska Landsmålen ock Svenskt Folkliv*, vol. 2 (1880–1887), 64.
[40] Piotr Wawrzeniuk, "En resande i svenskhet. Herman Vendell i Gammalsvenskby 1881," *Personhistorisk tidskrift* (2009): 2, 151, 155.

during the nineteenth century. They often cooperated with the Church, or with governmental authorities in the town and rural districts. As the industrialization and urbanization process gained momentum up towards the end of the nineteenth century, the main thrust of attention of the activists was directed towards the workers in towns, rather than, as earlier, the poor in the rural areas. The social question was in no way unique to Sweden but was the subject of a heated debate in many other countries, too. Those in Sweden who wished to help the poor often sought to benefit from the experiences of countries that had industrialized earlier, notably Germany and Great Britain.[41] For Gammalsvenskby, the activities of Emma Skarstedt, who was sent to the village by *Kvinnliga Missions Arbetare* (Female Missionary Workers), proved very important. She finally married into the village, becoming the wife of the village teacher Christoffer Hoas, the future pastor.

The modernizers from outside

The visit of Herman Vendell in the summer of 1881 started a wave of interest in the village. This section shows how his convictions influenced the choice of what to study, see and describe in Gammalsvenskby. Vendell's visit took place at a time when mass nationalism was on the rise in Finland and Sweden and a broad public sphere came into being. One of the most notable features of the latter was emergence of the press. Vendell's accounts of the village would hardly have gained such attention, if they had only reached the narrow circle of *Svekoman* activists in Helsinki. He published stories about Gammalsvenskby already whilst he was in the village. His essays continued to appear in the press for over a year. It was not only the journals where Vendell published his articles that spread the news about Gammalsvenskby, other journals also picked up his stories in a snowball effect and word of his findings reached further afield. Some of them remained interested in the village for a considerable period of time. Vendell's writings had almost an immediate impact on the readership of national-minded Swedes and Swedophone inhabitants of Finland, and facilitated fund raising for the village in Finland, Sweden, and among Swedes in the USA. In newspapers and journals, the story of the villagers' attachment to Swedish culture was repeated along with warnings of their impending assimilation, if Gammalsvenskby was not given sufficient assistance.

---

[41] Roddy Nilsson, "Den sociala frågan," in *Signums svenska kulturhistoria. Det moderna genombrottet*, ed. Jakob Christensson (Stockholm: Signum, 2008), 141–143, 158.

Herman Vendell visited Gammalsvenskby in the summer of 1881; he viewed his journey as a completion of his earlier expeditions between 1877 and 1879, when he collected samples of dialects in Swedophone enclaves in the Russian provinces of Estonia and Livonia.[42] After arriving in the village, Vendell swiftly proceeded to describing the interethnic relations. The relationship between the villagers and Germans from the neighboring villages had been deteriorating. The Germans have "forced upon" the Swedes a "hated" German teacher. They also wanted the Swedes to participate in, and co-finance, the construction of a new church that would be situated between two German Protestant villages. According to Vendell, the resistance against the latter was fierce. The villagers of Gammalsvenskby begged Vendell to help to bring a Swedish priest to them and a teacher who would master the Swedish language.[43]

Although Vendell's role, which he had created for himself, was to collect samples of the Gammalsvenskby/Dagö dialect, he considered it only natural to also study and describe the physiognomy of the villagers; it unequivocally proved their Swedish, and Germanic roots. "The Swedish type immediately steps before one's eyes – naturally, as there are no mixed marriages. There are several beauties among the women," Vendell wrote. The villagers were also quick when it came to making decisions and passing judgments, enthusiastic socializers, and they were industrious. Although they were "happy with their lot in life," they still thought of "Svenskland" (approximately "Swedeland"), as they called Sweden. To Vendell, the villagers of Gammalsvenskby appeared to be of the same "flesh and blood" as Swedophones in Finland; he added that he had never seen "more upright or friendlier characters."[44]

Vendell's accounts of his journey appeared in *Folkwännen* (literally: "Friend of the People"), a Helsinki weekly in 1881, and a cultural-scientific monthly *Finsk tidskrift* in 1882. The articles shaped the image of the village among the Finnish, later also Swedish, readership for a long time to come. After describing the lack of a Swedish priest and teacher (the children were taught in German) in the village (the former task being carried out by the bell-ringer of the village, "a simple peasant"), Vendell struck a somber tone. "Our kinsmen," he wrote, "are in danger of national obliteration at the

---

[42] SLS FS, SLS 182c, "Berättelse öfver den resa, hvilken sommaren 1881 företogs till Gammal-Svenskby ock Nargö af Herman Vendell, Docent" (Docent Herman Vendell's account of his journey to Gammalsvenskby and Nargö in the Summer of 1881), p. 1/68.
[43] SLS 182c, p. 21/88-22/89, citations p. 21/88.
[44] SLS 182c, p. 27/94-28/95.

hands of Germans and Russians." The situation was urgent, and called for a Swedophone man who could perform church services, and teach the children in Swedish. One-hundred and twenty *desiatinas* of land, three hundred roubles annually, and free accommodation were promised by the villagers to such person. In fact, Vendell continued, Gammalsvenskby should enjoy the same degree of support as the Swedes of Estonia and Livonia had received recently thanks to the Finnish Church's consistories and the Swedish Evangelical Foundation (*Svenska Evangeliska Fosterlands Stiftelsen*).[45]

In 1899, the association *Kvinnliga Missions Arbetare* decided it would send Emma Skarstedt to Gammalsvenskby. With several years' teaching experience, and a good knowledge of German (the villagers were reported to speak Swedish, German and Russian), she was regarded as the most suitable candidate to become a teacher of handicrafts, and function as a "Bible woman."[46] Needless to say, the association's most fundamental aim was that she would fulfill the latter function.

From her first days in the village, Skarstedt reported about poverty, the poor health conditions, and various aspects of village life that she considered archaic or even superstitious. She found the economic situation of many villagers hard. Several had to borrow money to be able to pay their taxes. Cash was borrowed at high interest rates that could bring ruin upon many households.[47] In the summer of 1900, Skarstedt wrote that the three main problems of the village were drunkenness, religion, and the ongoing strife about the distribution of the economic aid that the village had received. It was difficult to promote temperance in a milieu where many believed that abstaining from drink "was synonymous with belonging to some sects." In the sphere of religion, she noted, most believed that the mere fact of being a Lutheran would secure one's salvation. In addition, the villagers would not use the correct Swedish adjective for Lutheran ("luthersk"), but insisted on saying "luthérisk," a word that sounded ridiculous to a modern Swede like Skarstedt. Moreover, the villagers could not tell the difference between religions.[48] What emerges from her reports is a group of people who had been spared the campaign of the Swedish

---

[45] Herman Vendell, "Från svenskar i Ryssland," *Folkwännen*, no. 27 (1881).
[46]*Hemåt* 1899: 6–7 (juni-juli), p. 76; *Hemåt* 1899: 11 (November), p. 11. *Hemåt* was a journal, the tribune of Kvinnliga Missions Arbetare (Female Mission Workers) and Swedish branch of *KFUK* (*Kristliga föreningen av unga kvinnor*, Christian Young Women's Association). Journal of the Female Missionary Workers, Sweden.
[47]*Hemåt*, (1900): 2, februari.
[48]*Hemåt*, (1900): 8–9 (September), p. 92.

Church against the remnants of Roman Catholic beliefs among the population in the seventeenth and first half of the eighteenth century. The belief (or practices that suggested such a belief existed) that our salvation depended on our deeds in our life on earth was particularly common.[49] A non-Lutheran missionary who also visited Gammalsvenskby, Wilhelm Sarwe, saw Skarstedt struggling with various beliefs among the villagers, but also with their distrust. Several believed she intended to re-baptize them, only because she would teach people the song *Få vi mötas där vid floden* ("Let us meet down at the River…").[50] To make things worse, the authorities found Skarstedt's work dubious, and threatened to deport her. Skarstedt's lack of success in the sphere of temperance and religiosity brought her to the brink of exhaustion. She left for Sweden to rest and to attend nursery school before taking on the great challenges she realized lay ahead.[51]

No missionary work and no religious enlightenment were possible without an introduction of a minimum of modern health care in the village. In 1903, Skarstedt reported that the villagers could only "be reached by the Gospel" by indirect means. Organizing basic health care could help. Once the physical health of the villagers improved, measures could be taken to engage them in the conscious and active form of religiosity represented by Skarstedt. Although such measures were beyond the purview of what *Kvinnliga Missions Arbetare* normally approved of, Skarstedt was permitted to engage in such work, as it was deemed crucial "to keep our work over there going."[52] Having been left to their own devices, the villagers employed methods that were so superstitious and revolting that to be able to believe "that something like that can go in a Christian country" one had to see it oneself." The tradition of "reading" over the sick could perhaps be viewed as normal, if God's words were used. Instead, Skarstedt found various "heathen" influences. A rat's head baked in bread, a snake's head tied around the neck, and dung were other folk medicines that the missionary found revolting. The problem was also that the villagers deeply believed in the abilities of the so-called "wise women" (*kloka gummor*, a sort of naturehealers) to treat the sick, and called for Skarstedt (since her return to the village in 1902 as a nurse with a diploma) only as a last resort – often when

---

[49] Göran Malmstedt, *Bondetro och kyrkoro: religiös mentalitet i stormaktstidens Sverige* (Lund: Nordic Academic Press, 2002).
[50] Wilhelm Sarwe, *Bland Rysslands folk: i missionens och Röda korsets tjänst 1882–1922*, vol. 3, *Gammalsvenskby* (Stockholm: Svenska Missionsförbundet, 1929), 42–45, 50.
[51] Alvin Isberg, *Svensk lutherdom i österled. Relationer till ryska och baltiska diasporaförsamlingar och minoritetskyrkor (1883–1941)* (Uppsala University, 1982), 23.
[52] *Hemåt*, (1903): 8 (oktober), p. 100.

it was too late. This was hardly surprising, wrote Skarstedt, as the villagers for a very long time could only depend on themselves for help. No wonder, she added, "if they were somewhat behind their time."[53]

Emma Skarstedt's work mirrored the religious modernization that had been underway in Sweden since the early eighteenth century. After the introduction of religious freedom in the mid-nineteenth century, various churches competed for followers. People were supposed to develop a personal relationship to God - a form of religiosity that was very different from the automaton-like religiosity that Skarstedt meant was typical of many of the villagers. At the same time, her mission represented the entrance of the Swedish social movement into the village; the task of the modernizers was to teach people to help themselves. From Skarstedt's point of view, the village was in urgent need of spiritual and material help. Vendell, on the other hand, was driven by motifs that were both patriotic and romantic. His enthusiastic belief in the patriotism of the villagers was due to the fact that they had by and large preserved their language and most elements of their culture, and that belief functioned as a romantic filter through which everything he knew or read about the Gammalsvenskby passed. Where Skarstedt saw misery and problems, Vendell saw a reservoir of edifying examples to be used on the "home front" – in Finland, where the Swedophone minority was beginning to feel the pressure from the Finnish majority that was claiming political and cultural rights.

The lost Swedish tribe

There were critical voices among the Swedish visitors to the village. Skarstedt's view was to some extent shared by Viktor Hugo Wickström (newspaper editor, writer, and liberal politician), Anton Karlgren (a linguist and journalist) and Herman Neander (a Lutheran priest) who visited the village before the First World War. They too dwelled on the patriotism of the villagers on the one hand, but – unlike Vendell – they also took up issues they considered problematic. In the end, the image of the village as unyieldingly patriotic and genuinely Swedish remained more or less intact up to 1929 when most of the villagers migrated to Sweden. The myth of genealogy, as this point of view can be called, survived more or less intact, although there were dissenting voices among Swedish public and publicists in 1920s, when the future fate of the villagers was discussed. However, those

---

[53]*När och Fjärran* (1904): 1, 6; *Hemåt* (1902): 7, 83. *När och Fjärran* was issued as a supplement to *Hemåt* from 1904.

were largely set aside in the process of the bringing of the villagers to Sweden.[54]

The myth of genealogy is a powerful tool for holding nations together. It defines the nation as an emotional category rather than a legal rational one.[55] For the purpose of this text, a myth can be characterized as "widely shared assumptions, often unspoken and unconscious," maintained by stereotypes, images, and metaphors.[56] The various elements of a myth should be easily understood by a group it addresses, and it usually contains evocation of the past as guidance for the future. A myth in this context is not synonymous with a lie; however, the facts it contains have usually been selected to suit the intentions of its creators. Mass media have been identified as a main source of myth-like structures in recent times.[57]

The nationalistic-romantic view of history was most explicit in the Swedophone Finnish press, but there was also an exchange of information and ideas between the Finnish and the Swedish press. Gammalsvenskby was a valuable asset in the ever growing stream of news; stories of the village were attention-grabbing and sensational whilst at the same time tapped into a (perceived) cultural and mental proximity. The village was frequently presented as something astounding (a tiny group of people preserving their culture in hostile surroundings), and in this era of intense nationalism readers could easily identify with Swedophones far away. Where the developments in Gammalsvenskby were concerned the liberal and conservative press shared a "consensual paradigm" with their readership. The term refers to consensus on how the world should be viewed.[58]

In the case of Gammalsvenskby, the paradigm was patriotic, romantic and inclusive. This approach was predated by the writings of August Sohlman in the mid-nineteenth century. A liberal publisher and editor, he wrote a booklet on the history of the Estonian Swedes in terms very similar to those used by Vendell. The interest in "the smaller branches [of the Swedish people] that had been broken away from the mother stem" was "heartening," as they had

---

[54] Anna Wedin, *Gammalsvenskbybornas emigration till Sverige 1929. En studie i svenskhet och etniskt ursprung*, Bachelor Thesis at Södertörn University, 2007.
[55] Chris Rojek, *The Brit Myth. Who Do Britons Think They Are* (London: Reaktion Books Ltd, 2007), 75.
[56] Vejas Gabriel Liulevicius, *The German Myth of the East* (Oxford: Oxford University Press, 2009), 3.
[57] Piotr Cichoracki, *Legenda i Polityka. Kształtowanie się wizerunku marszałka Józefa Piłsudskiego w świadomości zbiorowej społeczenstwa polskiego w latach 1918–1939* (Kraków: Księgarnia Akademicka, 2005), 9-10.
[58] Gunilla Lundström, *När tidningarna blev moderna. Om svensk journalistik 1898–1969* (Lund University, 2004), 23-24.

preserved "their ancient nature and state." By studying them, the Swedes could learn "to understand their disposition, character and vocation in world history." To Sohlman, the Estonian Swedes possessed qualities from olden times, qualities that had now on the whole been lost by the Swedish peasantry, who had undergone a "common national development," with "good and bad" consequences.[59] Two statements are important for this text: there were edifying examples to be found in the past that had been preserved by the Estonian and Livonian Swedes; some of these superior qualities had disappeared from Sweden proper owing to the process of modernization, a phenomenon where "national development" can definitely be included. The common ancestry was understood to outweigh the differences that had arisen over time. The words "stem" and "tribe" are same in Swedish ("stam"), and thus, the phrase "mother tribe" comes to one's mind.

The rhetoric of something long since lost and then miraculously recovered surfaces frequently in the descriptions of the village. In practically all of the texts read by the author of this chapter, the ancient nature of the village's customs is stressed along with the patriotism of the villagers. Therefore, it was argued, they deserved financial aid and moral support. The villagers quickly learned this useful discourse, and as early as in 1883, with the helping hand of Kristian Wahlbeck from Finland petitioned their "kinsfolk" in Sweden and elsewhere to support the ongoing church construction.[60] Wahlbeck had answered Vendell's call for a Swedish-speaking village teacher and moved to Gammalsvenskby. He wrote letters that were published in the Finnish press, and toured Finland to collect funds in 1883; similar campaigns were undertaken in Sweden and among Swedes in the USA. Most illustrative was the call for "the fellow Christians and kinsfolk in the Kingdom of Sweden" to make donations to the construction of a church, first published in *Folkwännen* in 1883. The villagers also described themselves as "living in the southern lands among Germans and Russians," underlining their remoteness, isolation, their status as a minority thereby – indirectly – conjuring up an image of something lost, displaced, in need of help.[61] This image of remoteness and isolation, along with the villagers' "faithfulness" to the Swedish language and "devotion" to their ancient customs was frequently evoked. *Folkwännen* praised the "faithfulness" of the inhabitants of Gammalsvenskby to the Swedish

---

[59] August Sohlman, *Om lemningarne af svensk nationalitet uti Estland och Liffland* (Stockholm: published by the author, 1852), 1–3.
[60] *Folkvännen*, no. 103, 7 maj 1883, "Gammal-Svenskby."
[61] *Folkvännen*, no. 285, 6 december 1883, "Ännu engång Gammal-Svenskby."

language.⁶² *Kotka Nyheter* informed their readership that the villagers had "faithfully" preserved their language, religion and customs "among alien peoples, as if ship-wrecked on an island in the open sea."⁶³ In an article discussing the likelihood of the Swedish-speaking population of Finland adopting the Finnish language and Finnish customs, *Åbo tidning* described Gammalsvenskby as an elevating example of the perseverance and conservatism of Swedophone peasants in general. The author, who called himself "Yeoman" (*Allmogeman*), claimed that this was impossible, given the conservatism and a sense of superiority towards the Finns manifest among the Swedophones.⁶⁴ *Nya Pressen* cited the pastor of the Swedish parish in St Petersburg, H. Kajanus, who called for financial aid to Gammalsvenskby after the bad harvest of 1899, and claimed that "they [the villagers] do really not deserve to be forgotten" as their religion and traditions had been preserved so well.⁶⁵ The above examples from the Finnish press illustrate a genealogy myth in making, on its way to function automatically by evoking certain images and emotions without further scrutiny. Starting from Herman Vendell's first letter to Folkwännen and continuing with the letters supposedly written by the villagers to their "kinsfolk," we witness the beginning of imagining of the village as a Diaspora. This is evidenced by the viable cultural and financial links and the process of interaction between the villagers and the well-willing outsiders where the concepts of village's Swedishness were now created.

In general, the Swedish visitors did not ignore the fact that the Swedes of Gammalsvenskby had been influenced by the surrounding society in one way or another. However, such influences were more often than not viewed as corrupting. Anton Karlgren claimed that whilst the Germans, who arrived in 1805, "saved" the Swedes from becoming "savages" following their extended isolation, they also started a long-term cultural and material (the land originally reserved for the Swedish colonists) conflicts.⁶⁶ Herman Neander mentioned the corrupting influence of the authorities, who permitted the opening of an inn in the village. The German "seizure" of land that had originally belonged to the Swedes eventually made several Swedish villagers into paupers. This had a corrupting influence on their morals and the end result could be that they migrated and lost their national

---

⁶²*Folkwännen*, no. 64, 18 mars 1886, "Bref från Gammal-Svenskby."
⁶³*Kotka Nyheter*, no. 60, 24 december 1897.
⁶⁴*Åbo Tidning*, nr. 67, 10 mars 1889, "Bref från landsbygden."
⁶⁵*Nya Pressen*, no. 27, 29 januari 1900.
⁶⁶ Karlgren, *Gammalsvenskby*, 9–12.

character. The problem was made worse by the local custom of finalizing transactions by drinking vodka. The villagers had furthermore developed an unhealthy custom of lavish spending at wedding parties, something that not only seemed immoral, but also brought economic ruin upon several families who borrowed money for such festivities. Neander also cited extensively from a letter full of words borrowed from Russian. The letter was written by a young man from the village who was doing his military service in the Russo-Japanese war.[67] Victor Hugo Wickström, who visited the village in 1897, found the villagers prone to drink. According to him, the Russian authorities were to blame, since they ignored the protests that had been made and opened an inn in the village.[68] In other words: the Swedish core was good and genuine, but, in the long run, it was threatened by the contacts with the surrounding world.

Conclusions

The main aim of this chapter has been to study how the image of Gammalsvenskby was formed and maintained from 1881 to 1914. The main proposition was that the village was largely a creation by visitors to Gammalsvenskby during the three decades preceding the First World War. The visitors, in their turn, were affected by rapid developments in Finland and Sweden, cultural differentiation being the single most important feature. What the visitors encountered was a village where many aspects typical of the peasantry of the early modern period had been preserved – such as a strong attachment to religion, traditional customs, and loyalty towards the Crown, as well as great respect for elders and oral tradition. What the visitors saw was a village that basically did not differ from the villages inhabited by Swedophones in the Russian province of Estonia, in Finland and in Sweden. The romantic and nationalistic sentiments prevailed, and – although the criticism towards the developments viewed as negative by several of the visitors was not lacking – these inclusive schemes had the upper hand. The visit of Herman Vendell, the Svekoman linguist from Finland, was the starting point of the creative process. From Vendell's reports in the Finnish press, the myth of genealogy that linked the village to Swedophone Finland, Estonia and to Sweden was beginning to form. The

---

[67] Neander, *Gammal-Svenskby*, 3–41.
[68] Victor Hugo Wickström, *I öster- och västerled. Reseminnen* (Östersund: Jämtlandspostens boktryckeri, 1900), 31. The author also published his accounts in his newspaper, *Jämtlandsposten*.

villagers also swiftly learned the new discourse. However, during the process, the fact that the villagers had been influenced by developments in southern Russia for more than a hundred years was largely ignored, and only the historical and cultural features that seemed integrating were adopted. This meant that the features acquired during the long-term socialization in the specific milieu of the steppe were largely ignored. The similarities mattered, while the differences that were also found were not ascribed the same weight. The myth of genealogy proved strong. Thus it was only after the villagers had migrated to Sweden in 1929 that it was realized that many of them did not have the skills and mental faculties expected from a modern Swede.

Little Red Sweden in Ukraine
– the 1930s Comintern project in Gammalsvenskby

Soon the brothers will see the East in the Gold

Swedish Communist Party's slogan
May Day 1931

ANDREJ KOTLJARCHUK

The history of Gammalsvenskby offers a unique opportunity to investigate totalitarian political techniques in the twentieth century. The Swedish agricultural colony on the bank of the river Dnipro, not far from its fall into the Black Sea, is the only Scandinavian settlement in Eurasia. The church of Gammalsvenskby was the first Lutheran parish in the Azov and Black Sea territories. It functioned from 1782 to 1929. They owned the plots they cultivated and as foreign colonists they had a considerable degree of self-government in the Russian Empire and Soviet Ukraine.[1]

Recent research shows that the colonists of Gammalsvenskby had a high degree of ethnic self-consciousness. They considered themselves Swedes and spoke Swedish fluently in its dialect and standard form.[2] Since the middle of the nineteenth century the inhabitants of the village were in continuous contact with the Kingdom of Sweden and ethnic Swedes of the Grand Duchy of Finland. A number of Swedish cultural institutions (e.g., school, new church, library and choir) were erected or founded thanks to

---

[1] Svetlana Bobyleva, "Shvedy i gosudarstvennaia vlast Ukrainy," in *Voprosy germanskoi istorii*, ed. Svetlana Bobyleva (Dnepropetrovsk: Porogi, 2008), 247268.
[2] Anton Karlgren, *Gammalsvenskby: land och folk, serie: svenska landsmål och svenskt folkliv* (Uppsala, 1929); Alexander Mankov, "Selo Staroshvedskoe (Gammalsvenksby) i ego dialekt. Rezultaty issledovanii 2004–2006 gg.," in *Shvedy: sushchnost i metamorfozy identichnosti*, ed. Tamara Torstendahl-Salycheva (Moskva: RGGU, 2008), 294–314.

the Scandinavian aid given to the village. As a consequence the colonists received "an inoculation" of modern Swedish nationalism.³

During the first half of the twentieth century, this tiny Swedish community became the subject of a series of social experiments conducted by different political regimes. Their aim was to change the collective identity of the colonists and make them to the new authorities. Under the guidance of the Ukrainian *Tsentralnyi Komitet natsionalnykh menshyn* (TsKNM) a policy of "indigenization" was conducted between 1923 and 1929 with the aim of transforming the former foreign colonists of the Russian Empire into a loyal ethnic minority of Soviet Ukraine.⁴ After virtually the whole village (888 persons) had moved to their historic fatherland under the control of the "Gammalsvenskbykommittén" (Old-Swedish Village Committee) that had been formed in Sweden, a new large-scale experiment was undertaken between 1929 and 1938. The aim of this experiment was to fully integrate the "archaic" Ukrainian Swedes into the modern Swedish society by transforming them into successful Swedish farmers. The emigrants were denied a separate settlement in Sweden and the "Old Swedes" were spread all over the country to undergo "instruction in the Swedish norms of economic and every day activities."⁵ Inspectors appointed by the Committee monitored all aspects of the integration of the "lost generation" into the Swedish society. The colonists who disagreed with this policy (around 265 persons) returned to the USSR in 1930–1931. There, in so-called Röd Svenskby (Red Swedish Village), an experiment was launched which aimed to create the first Swedish *kolkhoz* and village council in the USSR. It was conducted under the patronage of the Comintern and supervision of Swedish Communists and lasted for five years. This chapter constitutes the first scientific account of this short-lived and ill-fated endeavor.

---

³ Piotr Wawrzeniuk, "En resande i svenskhet. Herman Vendell i Gammalsvenskby 1881," *Personhistorisk tidskrift* 2009:2, 149–164; Tatiana Shrader, "Ocherki zhizni shvedskikh kolonistov v Rossii 19 veka," in *Skandinavskie chteniia 2006* (St Petersburg: Nauka, 2008), 229–253.
⁴ About the politics of indigenization see: Harold R. Weinstein, "Language and Education in the Soviet Ukraine," *Slavonic Year Book* 1 (1941): 124–148; James E. Mace, *Communism and the dilemmas of national liberation: national communism in Soviet Ukraine, 1918–1933* (Cambridge, Mass.: Harvard Ukrainian Research Institute, 1983), 215–217; Martin Terry, *The affirmative action empire: nations and nationalism in the Soviet Union, 1923–1939* (Ithaca: Cornell University Press, 2001).
⁵ Anna Wedin, "Gammalsvenskbybornas emigration till Sverige 1929. En studie i svenskhet och etniskt ursprung," Unpublished Bachelor Thesis in history supervised by Andrej Kotljarchuk (Södertörn University 2007), 2–23.

Sources

The protocols of the Swedish Communist Party, which are kept in *Arbetarrörelsens arkiv* (Labor Movement Archives of Sweden KOLLA), document the discussions of the party on the measures to be taken by the party in relation to the ideological work among the Ukrainian Swedes in the years 1929–1931. The relevant collection for this research is Biografica which includes biographies of the activists who worked in Gammalsvenskby. Access to the material was granted by the executive committee of the *Vänsterpartiet* (The Left Party of Sweden). At *Riksarkivet* (National Archives of Sweden), two sets of documents are particularly interesting: firstly, the materials of *Socialstyrelsen* (National Board of Health and Welfare of Sweden), which contain correspondence with the villagers, lists of the persons who returned to the USSR, documents of *Gammalsvenskbykommittén* (Old-Swedish Village Committee) and *Arbetarnas Svenskbykommitté* (Workers' Swedish Village Committee), documents from the Soviet Consulate in Stockholm; and, secondly, the archives of the Ministry for Foreign Affairs of Sweden containing materials dated 1930–1933 from the Swedish Embassy in Moscow on the situation in the village, correspondence dated 1932–1933 on the question of bringing back Swedish communists and some other villagers from the USSR to Sweden, and a collection of Soviet and Swedish newspaper publications about the Old Swedes.

The archives of the Communist International at the Russian State Archive for Social and Political History include the personal files of the communists who worked in Gammalsvenskby.[6] Thanks to the powers of attorney of the relatives residing in Sweden the author gained access to the most important part of these files where he found the file "O staroshvedskikh poseleniiakh na Ukraine" (About the Swedish Settlements in Ukraine). This confidential file, which was created by the officials of the *Skandinaviska ländersekretariatet* (Secretariat for Scandinavian countries), contains different materials highlighting the Comintern's policies towards Gammalsvenskby.[7]

In the vast collection of material on the history of Gammalsvenskby kept at the State Archives of Kherson Oblast, the 1933 criminal case 287 by GPU of the Ukrainian SSR on accusing the group of the Old Swedes and Swedish communists in the organizing of mass re-emigration to Sweden is of great

---

[6] RGASPI, f. 495 "Ispolnitelnyi komitet Kominterna," 1919–1943, op. 275 "Lichnye dela. Kommunisticheskaia partiia Shvetsii" (Personal files. Communist Party of Sweden).
[7] RGASPI, f. 495, op. 31, d. 153.

value. Based on the powers of attorney on behalf of the relatives, the author was given authorization to work on this criminal case.

The author also has used materials from the Swedish mass media, as well as central Soviet and regional Ukrainian newspapers, and in addition to that also a variety of publications and documents about the Old Swedes

Theoretical framework

By applying the thought of Michel Foucault and Alberto Melucci, the author intends to study the techniques used by the Comintern and the Soviet state to force normalization upon the population that remained in the village. Their goal was to reshape the collective identity of Ukrainian Swedes and to prevent them from offering collective resistance to this process. The techniques of forced normalization are used in a process that can be divided into three phases: conceptualization, implementation, and results. Each phase has its own specific motives and mechanisms that influence the three following dimensions: 1) the configuration of new borders (administrative and geographical, social and political, historical, cultural); 2) the new normative standard (political, social and economical, cultural and linguistic); 3) the emergence of new collective values (through propaganda, education, work practices, cultural life, compulsory political rituals and so on).

The difference between the "old" identity standard and the new requirements causes conflicts in the collective identity and brings about changes in it.[8] The conditions of the totalitarian state intensify the technological effect by not granting the common actors any choice and making them participate in the project. According to Foucault, it is low efficient to look for the explicit logically ordered economic purposes in the activities of the authority. Each of the political regimes has their own different technologies, but only one common purpose of submission and the only one common and most popular method of violence. The format of this chapter does not make it possible to analyze more in detail all the aspects of the forced normalization. The research is focused on analyzing configuration of the new

---

[8] Michel Foucault, *Discipline and Punish. The Birth of the Prison* (New York: Vintage Books, 1979); *Power, Knowledge: Selected Interviews and Other Writings 1972–1977*, ed. Colin Gordon (New York: Pantheon, 1980); *The essential Foucault: Selections from Essential Works of Foucault, 1954–1984*, ed. Paul Rabinow and Nikolas Rose (New York: New Press, 2003); Alberto Melucci, "The process of collective identity," in *Social movements and culture*, under redaction, ed. Hank Johnson and Bert Klandermans (Minneapolis: University of Minnesota Press, 1995), 41–63.

borders and strategies of the collective resistance. Foucault viewed the strategies of collective resistance as the less studied part of forced normalization. Foucault notes that the resistance does not express viable alternative outside the power, but is a part of collaboration of the interaction between power and its subjects in order to function furthermore.[9]

The main political actors

The Comintern and the Swedish Communist Party

In 1926, the Comintern created a special secretariat, the Secretariat for Scandinavian countries, to facilitate communications with the Scandinavian communist parties, and to monitor, to report on and control the implementation of the resolutions of the Executive Committee of the Comintern. The Secretariat, remained active until 1935, was used to strengthen the control of the ECCI over the communist parties of Sweden, Norway, Denmark and Iceland.[10]

The imposition of its power by the Comintern was one of the main reasons for the division of the Swedish Communist Party in the fall of 1929; the most serious one in the history of the movement in Sweden. The split was a catastrophe for the communists loyal to the Comintern. Hugo Sillén, who led the pro-Comintern fraction, retained only 4,000 out of the 16,000 members of the SKP. The pro-Comintern party members lost the publishing house *Frams Förlag*, the leading communist newspaper *Folkets Dagblad Politiken*, most of its syndicates, and all communist members of parliament. The majority of the party followed Karl Kilbom into a new Swedish Communist Party, independent from the Comintern.[11] However, with financial aid from the Comintern, the SKP could regain its base and the mass media. From 1930 the pro-Comintern faction had at its disposal the

---

[9] Espen Schaanning, *Fortiden i våre hender: Foucault som vitenshåndtør*, vol. 1 (Oslo: Unipub, 2000), 357–360.
[10] Lars Björlin, "För svensk arbetarklass eller sovjetisk utrikespolitik? Den kommunistiska rörelsen i Sverige och förbindelserna med Moskva 1920–1970," in *Sovjetunionen och Norden – konflikt, kontakt, influenser*, ed. Sune Junger and Bent Jensen (Helsingfors: FHS, 1997), 214 (201–225).
[11] Bernt Kennerström, "Sprängningen av Sveriges Kommunistiska Parti 1929" in *Från SKP till VPK – en antologi*, ed. Sven Olsson (Lund: Zenit, 1976), 82–105; Lars Gogman, *I skuggan av Stalin. Lokala konsekvenser av 1929 års sprängning av Sveriges Kommunistiska Parti*. Unpublished MA-thesis (Stockholm University, 1991), 2–13; Jan Bolin, *Parti av ny typ?: skapandet av ett svenskt kommunistiskt parti 1917-1933* (Stockholm: Acta Universitatis Stockholmiensis, 2004), 368–369.

publishing house *Arbetarkultur*; the newspapers *Ny Dag*, *Norrskensflamman* and *Kalmar-läns Tidning*; the youth periodical *Stormklockan*; women's movement magazine *Arbetar-Kvinnornas Tidning*, a magazine attached to the communist women's movement; and the theoretical magazine *Kommunistisk Tidskrift*. The association *Sovjetunionens vänner* (Friends of the Soviet Union), which was controlled by the party, published its own magazine *Sovjetnytt*.

During the New Year vacation 1930–1931, a delegation from the SKP discussed the split of the party, as well as ways of getting out of the crisis, with the Comintern leaders. Sven Linderot and Paul Thunell were the heads of the Swedish delegation.

According to the Comintern, the Swedish Communist Party acted as a Social-Democratic one, "in isolation from the masses." Work among the peasantry in Sweden had never been under the influence of the Communists. But this fact was not taken into account by the Comintern.[12] The formal promoter of the Gammalsvenskby project was Allan Walenius – the director of the Comintern library and the head of the Scandinavian section at the *Kommunisticheskii universitet nationalnykh menshinstv Zapada imeni Markhlevskogo* (Markhlevskii Communist University of the National Minorities of the West). He had nightlong discussions with the Swedish communists about the bright future of Gammalsvenskby.[13] He was a very well educated man and one of the most influential theoreticians of communism in Scandinavia. In interwar Sweden, his articles on various issues related to socialism were published regularly.[14]

When the delegation returned to Sweden they brought with them a plan to make the agrarian population support the policy of the SKP:

> The agrarian question has not been taken into account. The party must obtain an agrarian program, and the work among agricultural workers and small farmers should be actively pursued.[15]

---

[12] Urban Lundberg, *En fokusering och tre punkter – en studie av SKPs försök att vinna arbetarklassen åt kommunismen under perioden 1929–1935*.Unpublished C-thesis in history (Stockholm University, 1994), 36–40.
[13] RGASPI, f. 495, op. 275, d. 284.
[14] Olof Mustelin, "Allan Wallenius - biblioteksman, publicist och revolutionär," in *Svenska litteratursällskapet i Finland:* 59 (Helsingfors, 1984), 269–389.
[15] Lundberg, *En fokusering*, 40–42.

Document 6: The report of the Secretariat for Scandinavian concerning the Old-Swedish immigrants in Sweden.

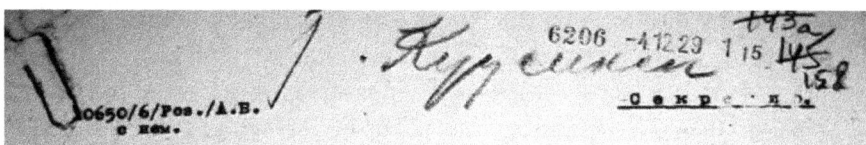

Source: Memorandum regarding the Ukrainian Swedes prepared by Aino Kuusinen, referent of the Skandinaviska ländersekretariatet for the leading staff of the Comintern, in RGASPI, f. 495, op. 31, d. 153.

Therefore, the former Gammalsvenskby villagers residing in Sweden became a testing ground for the agrarian work of the SKP. The protocols of

SKP's decision-making body, the political bureau, are not available for the years 1929–1932, as the party was in deep crisis, and many members were persecuted by the secret police. However, the few available documents that are available prove that Gammalsvenskby played an important role in the politics of the new party. At least six of the fifteen members of the political bureau of the SKP, including the party leaders Hugo Sillén and Sven Linderot, took immediate part in the discussions on the Old Swedes.

On the party's initiative, a special committee was formed, Arbetarnas Svenskbykommitté, to work among the colonists and to spite the official, state-led committee. The communists Kasper Gustafsson, Hilmer Fredriksson, Carl Bengtsson and Gunnar Sedin formed part of it. The members of the committee were in contact with the Swedish authorities, and carried out active propaganda to involve colonists in Communist activities. In addition, candidates for party work and activists in the women's movement (Lydia Utas) were chosen among the former villagers. These people and party agitators went on tours around the country.[16] For example, on 14 May 1931, the Swedish colonist Johan Knutas held a speech along with the well-known party agitator Fritjof Lager in the park of the town of Spånga.[17]

Information material about the villagers' desire to get back to the USSR became a regular topic which appeared regularly in the Communist press, playing an important part in the debates with the publications of the Social Democrats and the Communists led by Karl Kilbom.[18] SKP issued an optimistic note to the Swedish colonists explaining the meaning of a collective farm – the *kolkhoz*:

> You ask if you get pigs and chickens and have them as your own. Of course, you will get them if you buy them. It is only the land that is collective. Not houses and gardens. You write about the

---

[16] ARAB, Vänsterpartiet Kommunisterna. Protokoll politbyrå 1927–1931. Vol. A 3:1. RE 5/1.
[17] ARAB. Gamla samlingen. Vol. 11737. Bild nr. XXL 1931:008. Affisch "Tillbaka till Sovjet-Unionen. Föredrag hålles torsdagen den 14 maj kl. 4 e. m. (Kristi himmelsfärdsdag) i Spånga Folkets park av svenskbybon Johan Knutas. Dessutom föredras Fritjof Lager över ämnet Sovjet-Unionens diktatur eller Sveriges demokrati. Diskussion."
[18] Jonas Ramstedt, "Utsugningsobjekt eller Stamfränder: rapporteringen om Ukraina-svenskar i vänsterpress 1929–1931, ur klass- och nationalitetssynpunkt," Unpublished Bachelor Thesis in historia. Supervised by Andrej Kotljarchuk (Södertörn University, 2007).

tractor. Now there are twenty tractors in Röd Svenskby. There are even those who can repair them/.../.[19]

On the initiative of the SKP the villagers made a formal request for a visa permitting them to return to the USSR. The Central Committee of the SKP sent a telegram to the Secretariat for the Scandinavian countries requesting them "to support an application for entry into the USSR and to emphasize the political value of the return of the Old Swedes to the Ukrainian Soviet Republic."[20] As a result, the adviser of the Secretariat for the Scandinavian countries Aino Kuusinen prepared a memorandum which was presented to several leading staff members of the Comintern.

For Comintern the Gammalsvenskby project was interesting not only because of its value for the SKP. The future Swedish *kolkhoz* was an ideal place to send young Swedish communists studying at Comintern schools. Information about successes of the socialist construction in the Röd Svenskby could be publicized abroad through the radio of and the printed press of the Comintern. That was the usual practice. A group of Scandinavian communists was sent by the Comintern to inform members of the collective fishery *Polarstjernen* (The Polar star), and the Norwegian national village of Tsypnavolok. The Norwegian communist newspaper "Nordland Arbeiderblad" published a series of articles about the wonderful life of the Soviet-Norwegian fishermen.[21] Many Nordic communists were working at the national Finnish *kolkhozes* of Ingria, Karelia and North Caucasus.

The Soviet government

As a result of the negotiations between the Swedish and Soviet governments and on the basis of decree number 83, dated 6 June 1929, of the political bureau of the Soviet Communist party, the whole population of the village moved to Sweden at the end of July 1929.[22] The information about their departure attracted international attention,[23] and roused hopes among the

---

[19] Jörgen Hedman, Lars Åhlander, *Historien om Gammalsvenskby och svenskarna i Ukraina* (Stockholm: Dialogos, 2003), 217.
[20] RGASPI, f. 495, op. 31, d. 153, l.158.
[21] Morten Jentoft, *De som dro østover. Kola-nordmennenes historie* (Oslo: Gyldendal, 2001), 87–114.
[22] *Politburo TsK RKP (b)-VKP (b). Povestka dnia zasedanii, 1919–1929*, t. 1 (Moskva: ROSSPEN, 2000), 696–697; Oleg Ken, Aleksander Rupasov i Lennart Samuelsson, *Shvetsiia v politike Moskvy 1930–1950* (Moskva: ROSSPEN, 2005), 34–35.
[23] See as example: "Swedish colonists return from Ukraine," *Berkeley Daily Gazette*, July 27, 1929, 2.

other ethnic minorities of Ukraine. In the fall of 1929 around 11,000 German colonists from southern Ukraine and the Crimea, after having sold all their belongings, went to Moscow where they approached the German and Canadian embassies about getting visas. As a result of the negotiations between Germany and the USSR at the end of 1929 around 6,500 German colonists and Mennonites were permitted to leave the USSR. The struggle of the German peasants was continued in 1930.[24] The Kremlin considered their case as a special kind of class struggle by German colonists and insisted that the Ukrainian authorities should stop the inflow of German colonists to Moscow. In February 1930 the issue of mass emigration was discussed in the plenum of the central committee of the Communist Party of Ukraine, which adopted a resolution on how "to neutralize those anti-Soviet activities."[25] Mass emigration of Ukrainian Poles to Poland in the winter of 1929–1930 could be prevented only by strengthening border controls. The Polish authorities correctly noted that there was a direct link between the Ukrainian Poles' wish to emigrate and "the organized mass emigration of the Swedish colonists."[26] That is why the return of the Swedes back to the USSR could be used as a powerful ideological tool in the anti-emigration propaganda. Indeed, one of the first articles in the Kherson newspapers covering this topic considered the return of the Swedes to the USSR to be a lesson for the German colonists.

On 5 January 1930, the leading newspaper of the Kherson region *Naddniprianska Pravda* published the news that the collectivization process was to be completed and the kulaks liquidated as a social class. According to the decision of the regional party committee all homesteads were to be collectivized by 1 March 1930. "We have time limits of less than two months, not a single hour, not a single minute should be wasted," wrote the newspapers to warn their readers.[27] However, the process of proved extremely difficult because of the strong resistance of the German colonists. In the reports of the GPU, the situation in the German colonies of southern

---

[24] Harvey L. Dyck, *Weimar Germany and Soviet Russia, 1926-1933: A Study in diplomatic instability* (London: Chatto & Windus, 1966), 163–174; Natalia Ostasheva, *Na perelome epokh. Mennonitskoe obshchestvo Ukrainy v 1914–1931* (Moskva: Gotika, 1998), 162–165. Both authors do not see the connection between the emigration moods of Soviet Germans in late 1929 with the mass emigration of Swedish colonists to Sweden.
[25] Viktor Chentsov, "Kollektivizatsiia" in *Nemtsy Ukrainy*, ed. Svetlana Bobyleva, t. 7 (Moskva: Obshchestvennaiia akademiia nauk rossiiskikh nemtsev, 2002), 101-105.
[26] Jan Bruski, "Bolshoi golod na Ukraine v svete dokumentov polskoi diplomatii i razvedki," *Europa* 6, no. 21 (2006): 106.
[27] *Naddniprianska Pravda*, January 5, 1930, 1.

Ukraine was described as very close to rebellion.²⁸ Spontaneous uprisings by women took place in one village after another and people refused to work. In the spring of 1930, many fields remained waste. The wide-spread corruption in the Stalinist state made it possible for the German colonists to use bribes to have deported relatives sent back to them from Siberia. Several false certificates were issued by local village soviets to the effect that people who had been deported were in fact poor peasants, not *kulaks*. The Ukrainian peasants thought that this showed that "the soviet authorities are afraid of Germans."²⁹

Under these circumstances, the benevolent foundation of a Swedish *kolkhoz* could be a powerful tool in Soviet propaganda. To illustrate this one could mention the resolution adopted by the political bureau of the VKP(b) on 21 June 1931 on the resettlement of 77 peasant families from Poland in Soviet Ukraine; this would be "very useful for organizing at least one good, even better model *kolkhoz* which would effectively undermine the propaganda of the bourgeois press in Poland."³⁰ Similar ideas were at work in a resolution on the creation of a Swedish *kolkhoz*. The idea to create model *kolkhozes* based on emigrant groups was not new. Since the mid-1920s there was an American kolkhoz in Tambov province.³¹ In 1932 there were circa thirty foreign *kolkhozes* in the USSR employing more than 5,000 immigrants.³²

The negotiations concerning the Old Swedes and their return to Soviet Ukraine were conducted by the Soviet ambassador to Sweden Alexandra Kollontai who had talks with the Prime Minister of Sweden Carl Gustaf Ekman and Foreign Minister Fredrik Ramel.³³ All practical matters in

---

²⁸ Andrea Graziosi, "Collectivisation, révoltes paysannes et politiques gouvernementales à travers les rapports du GPU d'Ukraine de février-mars 1930," *Cahiers du monde russe,* no. 35 (1994), 438–472.
²⁹ E. A. Solonchuk, "Raskulachivanie v nemetskikh natsionalnykh raionakh Odesskogo okruga: zima-vesna 1930 (po materialam spetssvodok okruzhnogo GPU v partiinye organy," in *Nemtsy Odessy i Odesskogo regiona* ed. Alfred Eisfeld (Odessa: Astroprint, 2003), 217–233.
³⁰ Oleg Ken and Aleksandr Rupasov, *Politbiuro TsK VKP (b) i otnosheniia SSSR s zapadnymi stranami,* vol. 1, 1928–1934 (St Petersburg: Evropeiskii Dom, 2000), 526–527.
³¹ Aleksandr Kurylev, "Opyt trudovoi deiatelnosti rossiiskikh re-immigrantov v selskom khoziaistve v 1920-e gody. Na primere Pervoi Irskoi kommuny re-immigrantov iz Ameriki," in *Problemy sotsialnogo i gumanitarnogo znaniia* (St Petersburg: European University Press, 1999), 403–437.
³² Anders Gustafson, *Svenska sovjetemigranter: om de svenska kommunisterna och emigrationen till Sovjetunionen på 1920- och 1930-talen* (Linköping: Nixon, 2006), 17.
³³ Alexandra Kollontai, *Diplomaticheskie dnevniki,* vol. 2, 1922–1940 (Moskva: Academia, 2001), 12–14, 42–43; TASS communiqué. *Izvestiya,* August 13, 1931. Alexandra Kollontai

connection with the re-emigration were the responsibility of Consul Vladimir Smirnov.[34] Viktor Kopp, an ethnic German from Crimea by origin and former Soviet ambassador to Sweden, prepared the report for the Kremlin about the Old Swedes.[35] Having gone through all aspects of the matter he proposed "That they should be allowed to return on the condition that funding was provided by the Swedish government." In the end, the Swedish government paid the costs of the return of the colonists back to the USSR.

The final decision about the re-emigration of the Old Swedes was taken at the very highest level. On 15 June 1930 the political bureau of the VKP(b) led by Stalin responded positively to Kollontai's request "about letting in 40 Swedish colonists."[36] However, those who had already become Swedish citizens were given a visa "only if they agreed to join a kolkhoz."[37]

The re-emigration by the Swedes became a hot topic in the Soviet mass media. TASS informed regularly about the circumstances of their return. This news was also covered by the leading newspapers *Izvestiia* and *Pravda* as well as newspapers of the Soviet Ukraine and special editions for the Soviet Germans.[38] The film studio *Sovkinozhurnal* produced a short documentary film in 1930 called "Obratno v SSSR" (Back to the USSR).[39] A tract called "Dva goda v Evrope. Pochemu krestiane sela Staroshvedskogo vernulis iz Shvetsii" (Two Years in Europe: Why the Villagers of Gammalsvenskby Returned from Sweden) was published. The Ukrainian filmmaker Alexander Dovzhenko found this topic so interesting that he planned

---

was half-Swedish by origin. Her mother Alexandra Massalin was a Swedish noblewomen from Eastern Finland, see: Hans Björkegren, *Ryska posten: de ryska revolutionärerna i Norden 1906–1917* (Stockholm: Bonnier, 1985), 113.

[34] Vladimir Smirnov (1876–1952) was an "old" Bolshevik and Soviet-Russian diplomat with Swedish as a second native language. His mother Wirginia Nygren was Finno-Swedish. Before the 1917 revolution he was a lecturer in Russian at Helsingfors University (Helsinki). He was married to Karin Strindberg, the daughter of the famous Swedish writer August Strindberg. Smirnov had good connections with in the 1930s Swedish political and cultural elite. See: Yurii Dashkov, *Ego znali pod imenem Paulson. Dokumentalnaia povest o V. M. Smirnove* (Moskva: Izdatelstvo politicheskoi literatury, 1984).

[35] Oleg Ken, Aleksander Rupasov and Lennart Samuelsson, *Shvetsiia v politike Moskvy*, note 37.

[36] *Politburo TsK RKP (b)-VKP (b). Povestka dnia zasedanii, 1930–1939* (Moskva, 2001), vol. 2, no. 128.

[37] RA, Socialstyrelsen, Handlingar angående utlänningsärenden 1920–1938. Handlingar rörande Gammalsvenskbyborna 1929–1931. F II:2. 1402.

[38] "Rückkehr schwedischer Emigranten ein Schlag gegen die pfäffische Konterrevolution," *Rote Zeitung*, September 5, 1931.

[39] RGAKFD, no. 2107, "Obratno v SSSR. Vystuplenie v dome krestianina gruppy shvedov-kolonistov vernuvshikhsia iz Shvetsii." Sovkinozhurnal no 4/267. 1930.

to make a film about the Old Swedes.⁴⁰ Thus, because of the powerful political forces involved, the return of a very limited number of Old Swedes to the USSR became a big international project.

Configuration of the new boundaries

A new historical canon and a new vision of the future

A series of publications from 1929–1931 illustrate how the international communist movement looked upon the past and future of the Swedish colony in Ukraine. All of these texts were first and foremost intended for those responsible for carrying out the new project, i.e., Swedish communists and Comintern employees.

In December 1929 an unknown author from the Comintern wrote a report called "Das Alt-Schwedische Dorf." According to his analysis, Gammalsvenskby was home to class struggles and exploitation. Rich peasants (Grossbauer) like Johan Buskas who owned large plots of land turned the poor peasants (Kleinbauer) into their farm-hands, making them work for next to nothing. They were assisted by the Lutheran pastor, who also belonged to the class of exploiters. The October Revolution 1917 put an end to this exploitation, and justice with regard to land ownership became the rule. The Soviet power liberated the poor Swedish peasants, but capitalistic Sweden turned them into slaves again:

> The land was distributed in the same proportions to all except the priest who was not given land. That was surely the reason for his stomach aches. That is why the pastor launched the propaganda about going to Sweden, but the kulaks were the most interested supporting faction in this matter. In Sweden the victims of the Swedish nationalist propaganda became slaves of the landowners. The Swedish working class and the Communist Party came to the rescue of the cheated peasants. Now the colonists are ready to go back to Ukraine by foot. If they are given permission to re-emigrate, the kolkhoz will be created there not only for Swedish dwellers of the village, also Germans and Jews will join. The new life will put an end to nationalism and will be based upon the principles of the working solidarity and fraternity.⁴¹

---

⁴⁰ Alexander Dovzhenko, *The poet as filmmaker. Selected writings,* ed. Marco Carynnyk (Cambridge: MIT press, 1973), 68.
⁴¹ "Das Alt-Schwedische Dorf," RGASPI, f. 495, op. 31, d.153, ll. 146–158.

On 23 January 1930 the political bureau of the SKP charged the propaganda group with the preparation and publishing of a brochure dedicated to the so-called "Svenskby affair." The political bureau thought this publication would "help our comrades to gain an understanding of those matters."[42] The book "Svenskbyskandalen" (The Swedish Village Scandal) was printed in 1930. The author of the book was Gustav Johansson, who was at the same time a leading left-wing journalist and the editor-in-chief of the newspaper *Ny Dag* (New Day). Johansson viewed the story of the village in the same way as the Comintern report did, through the prism of class struggle and in the light of the leading position of the clergy in the village. The first months the Old Swedes spent in Sweden were seen as an example of capitalist exploitation and bourgeois cynicism. However, notwithstanding their conservatism the poor colonists quickly realized they had made a mistake and declared their wish to go back to the USSR. They approached the SKP for help (in fact the party agitator was planning to make propaganda work among the Ukrainian Swedes). The party could not leave "the victims of the nationalist propaganda" to their fate and therefore created the Workers' Swedish Committee. Funds were raised for the purchase of a tractor. The first group of colonists had already gone back to Ukraine where "the world of the old tradition gave place today to a kolkhoz in Röd Svenskby, a small part of the great Soviet socialist construction."[43]

When all Old Swedes wishing to return were back in the village, a brochure to be used for ideological work "Dva goda v Evrope" (Two Years in Europe) was published. The author used an assumed name, Mikhail Vasilev; most probably it was Maria Andriievskaia, a journalist from the Soviet peasant magazine *Lapot*.[44] The style of the brochure was plain and simple, the booklet was cheap (3 kopecks only), and the print run was 150,000 copies. Apparently, the target audience was expected to be extremely large. The book contained a set of interviews by the author with three peasants who had come back, Greis Albers, Petter J. Knutas and Alvina Knutas. However, their names were russified. The book contained a lot of false information and errors. This was of no concern to the author, as the main purpose was to provide a clear Marxist account of the past, present and future of Gammalsvenskby. According to the author, the resettlers founded the Swedish colony as "life in

---

[42] ARAB. Vänsterpartiet Kommunisterna. Protokoll politbyrå 1927–1931. Vol. A 3:1. RE 5/1. Protokoll 7. February 23, 1930, f. 4.
[43] Gustav Johansson, *Svenskbyskandalen* (Stockholm: Arbetarkultur, 1930), 35.
[44] Ivan F. Masanov, *Slovar psevdonimov russkikh pisatelei, uchenykh i obshchestvennykh deiatelei*, t.1 (Moskva: Knizhnaia Palata, 1956), 229.

Sweden was hardly possible, one and a half centuries before famine and poverty had driven the first group of desperate and brave men from Sweden to Russia."[45] The colony became rich,

> if compared to an average Russian village, the Swedish colonists had their own hospital, school, library house and their own national minority village administration. However, notwithstanding this apparent prosperity an ardent class struggle was in evidence in the village. As here, within this little piece of the Soviet land the kulaks were extremely opposed to giving up.[46]

According to the author, the real reason for the Old Swedes to move back to Sweden had been the collectivization and the resistance to it of the kulaks. In fact, the resolution on the emigration and departure of the colonist from the USSR was adopted before the collectivization campaign was launched in the Kherson Oblast. The plan to emigrate was the work of "the agent of capitalists" pastor Hoas and supported by *kulaks*, a caste of well-to-do farmers. The author employed the commonplace Soviet propaganda theme of the class struggle. The emigration is considered as a special kind of class struggle, as a reaction of by the *kulaks* to collectivization. The *kulaks* also had their allies: the priest, religious members of the community and poor but evil men called *podkulachniki*.[47] The stay in Sweden is depicted in gloomy and exaggerated terms. The situation of a farm-hand in Sweden is almost the same as that of an animal. According to Petter J. Knutas, the landowner Axtorp made the Old Swedes drink water out of a drum filled with cows' urine. Knutas said that in Sweden his daughter gave birth in the farmyard without any obstetrical help, whilst in Gammalsvenskby all women gave birth at the local hospital. If necessary, they could stay there for a long time, and could afford not to work thanks to an allowance from the state for bringing up a child. In Sweden, the Gammalsvenskby Swedes became slaves living in inhuman misery, sleeping being their sole entertainment. Petter J. Knutas concludes: "I left Soviet Russia as a simple,

---

[45] Mikhail Vasilev (pseud.), *Dva goda v Evrope. Pochemu krestiane sela Staroshvedskogo vernulis iz Shvetsii* (Two Years in Europe.Why the Villagers of Gammalsvenskby Returned from Sweden) (Leningrad: Priboi, 1931), 4.
[46] Vasilev, *Dva goda v Evrope*, 4–5.
[47] *Podkulachnik* is a Stalinist neologism means – "a person aiding the kulaks." This political label was used in the 1930s to designate those poor and middle-wealthy farmers who sided with *kulaks* in their opposition to collectivization and therefore persecuted by the Soviet regime as class enemies.

ignoramus, but in Sweden I became a revolutionary."⁴⁸ The author emphasizes the fact that the Old Swedes had taken an active part in the communist movement while still in Sweden. For example, a column consisting of 100 Ukrainian Swedes took part in the May Day demonstration in Stockholm in 1931. Thus, according to the author, the return to the USSR was a conscious choice "move on from the old to the new, from the slavery under *kulaks* to the free life in the kolkhoz under the guidance of the Bolshevik Party."⁴⁹

The aim of the socialist construction they had engaged in was formulated in an address dated 20 August 1931 with the heading "To the workers of the Soviet Union and the whole world!" In all 180 Swedes promised "to correct a big mistake made under the influence of letters from the priest and propaganda by kulaks, and to struggle together with all other peasants for total collectivization, for the liquidation of kulaks as a class." Special emphasis was given to their wish to make the "bitter experience" of their emigration known among the workers of the USSR. In accordance with Soviet political culture at the time, the address ended with cheers for the party, its leader comrade Stalin and the world revolution of the proletariat. In this way, the creation of the *kolkhoz* was the price the Swedes had to pay for their mistake.⁵⁰

Following the return of the first group to the village, an international meeting was arranged on the premises of the club (in the building of the former Swedish Church) with the German and Jewish neighbors of the Swedes. The Swedish communist Paul Söderman ("comrade Lindroos") opened the meeting. He was followed by Petter J. Knutas, who had become a member of the Communist Party in Sweden. Both speakers repeated the main theses of the party instructions, and said they were confident that all colonists still remaining in Sweden, excluding the kulaks, would return to their Motherland. Petter J. Knutas said more specifically:

> Having been in Sweden for a short time, we have at first hand experienced what capitalist exploitation is. Now we truly understand that only the Soviet government and Communist Party are our friends /.../ We will do everything to help the party to correct the mistake we have committed.⁵¹

---

⁴⁸ Vasilev, *Dva goda v Evrope*, 11.
⁴⁹ Vasilev, *Dva goda v Evrope*, 14.
⁵⁰ Vasilev, *Dva goda v Evrope*, 16.
⁵¹ Jungsturm, "Tilky radvlada i kompartiia nashi druzi," *Nadniprianska Pravda*, January 21, 1930, 2.

Illustration 3: Two Years in Europe: Why the Villagers of Gammalsvenskby Returned from Sweden.

Source: Book cover of "Dva goda v Evrope. Pochemu krestiane sela Staroshvedskogo vernulis iz Shvetsii" (Leningrad: Priboi 1931). Note the straightforward visual pedagogy of the cover.

The same chord was struck in the short documentary film, "Obratno v SSSR" (Back to the USSR). The subtitles claimed that the Swedes wanted "to correct the mistake we made with the decision to go back to Ukraine with a view to creating the first Swedish kolkhoz."[52] Thus, Soviet propaganda put forward three main principles for the future organization of Röd Svenskby. Firstly, a kolkhoz as a non-alternative socio-economic basis for all Swedish villagers would be founded. It was to function as an outpost of solid collectivization. Secondly, a cultural revolution would be launched. The values and customs of traditional agrarian society must be uprooted. Thirdly, the Swedish Communist Party and the Comintern would assume the leading role in the construction of a new socialist Swedish village.

A new administrative and geographical landscape

An important instrument in Soviet policy was to give places new names, particularly if the old ones were connected with the ancient regime. The new names were symbolic ones and served the purpose of building a new Soviet identity. In 1924, the capital city of the former Russian Empire was renamed Leningrad, despite the fact that Lenin was not born there, nor had he studied there.[53] The old name of the city was associated with St Peter and the emperor Peter I. In the same year, Iuzovka, an industrial centre in southern Ukraine, which was named after the Welsh businessman and founder of the city John Hughes, was renamed Stalino. In 1926 the other centre of the southern Ukraine – Ekaterinoslav was renamed Dnipropetrovsk.[54] Since 1926, the Swedish name of the village, Gammalsvenskby, received official recognition and was used by the local authorities besides the Russian and the Ukrainian names of the village. However, the historical name included the adjective "old," and that was not suitable in the light of the ongoing construction of a new world. On 5 February 1931 the newspaper of the central committee of the Communist Party of Ukraine *Radianske selo* wrote that the Swedes had not come back to Ukraine to rebuild the historical Gammalsvenskby, but to create a modern Red Swedish Commune.[55] On 16 February the same newspaper wrote that the village soviet of Gammalsvenskby had decided to change the name of the village to Röd Svenskby (Red Swedish Village).[56] The Swedish communist

---

[52] RGAKFD, no. 2107, "Obratno v SSSR. Vystuplenie v dome krestianina gruppy shvedov-kolonistov vernuvshikhsia iz Shvetsii," *Sovkinozhurnal*, no. 4/267, 1930.
[53] Literally "City of Lenin."
[54] Literally "Glory of Catherine II."
[55] "Pane Hooz vasha sprava prohrana," *Radianske selo*, February 5, 1931.
[56] "Staro-Shvedske stae Chervono-Shvedskym," *Radianske selo*, February 16, 1931.

press used the new name of the colony.⁵⁷ On 21March 1931 communist newspaper *Ny Dag* published the article "Röda Svenskby är stadd i snabb utveckling" (Röd Svenskby is under rapid development) describing the successes of communist construction and the Soviet nationalities policy towards the Ukrainian Swedes. In letters to the Secretariat for the Scandinavian Countries, the secretary of the local branch of the party of Gammalsvenskby Edvin Blom gave as his address (in Russian): USSR, Berislav district, Red Swedish village.⁵⁸ The decision to change the name was taken by the authorities, but according to Soviet political culture the initiative should really have come from below. The very first time a new, revolutionary name appears is in the book "Two Years in Europe." In response to the final remark made by the author: "The address should be written ...Kherson region, Old-Swedish colony," the Swedish colonists are said to have replied confidently: "No, that's wrong; you should write Red Swedish *kolkhoz*."⁵⁹

However, the *kolkhoz* was instead named after the Swedish Communist Party. The choice of name was meant to emphasize the special status of the *kolkhoz*, the activities of which had been carried out under the auspices of the international communist movement. It should be noted that the new name of the village disappeared along with the international communist project and from 1934 to 1945 the historical name of the village Staroshvedskoe (Old-Swedish village) is used in all known sources.

The village was given its former administrative status as a national Swedish village council, the only one in Ukraine and the Soviet Union. This was a breach of Ukrainian law, as the minimum demographic norm for creating a national council was 500 persons.⁶⁰ The number of the Swedes, who came back to the USSR, including also the families of the Swedish communists who settled in the village, did not exceed 300 persons. The decision was dictated by the political importance of the project, as well as by the hope to attract new members to the Swedish colony. Between1930 and 1933, the Old Swedes who went back to the USSR maintained continuous contact with those who preferred to stay in Sweden. Up to 1932, the letters of the Soviet Swedes described the successes of the new life in the USSR and

---

⁵⁷ "Röda Svenskby är stadd i snabb utveckling," *Ny Dag*, Februari 21, 1931, 1; "Svensk sovjetarbetare berättar om Röda Svenskby just nu," *Ny Dag*, April 4, 1931, 1, 8; "Röda Svenskby hälsar SKP," *Ny Dag*, May 14, 1932, 1; "Kamrat Blom berättar om Sovjets land," *Stormklockan*, no. 7 (1932): 2.
⁵⁸ RGASPI, f. 495, op. 275, d. 341.Lichnoe delo. Hugo Albert Lauenstein.
⁵⁹ Vasilev, *Dva goda v Evrope*, 16.
⁶⁰ A. B. Glinskii, *Natsionalnye menshinstva na Ukraine* (Kharkov: Tsentrizdat, 1931), 31.

called upon the former Gammalsvenskby who were now in Sweden to return to their home. For example, Petter J. Knutas wrote the following in a letter to Andreas Annas (30November 1931):

> I live a hundred times better than I lived in Sweden. I am glad to be free from the Swedish plague. We work in our kolkhoz or *artel* as we call it. The damned priests continue to poison the people and those who are ignorant still believe them, but they will never deceive us again. We have a cinema with sessions four times a month and we pay only 7 rubles 50 kopecks from the whole village /.../ On the commemoration of the October Revolution we had a holiday, we organized a banquet in the church (roasted two calves), and then watched movies. We need more workers. Come back, because we are building socialism, even for those who remained in Sweden. Welcome home!
>
> Swedish Communist Party Kolkhoz Röd Svenskby.[61]

Creating a new hierarchy

The status of the national Soviet corresponded well with the policy of indigenization. Introduced in the USSR in 1923, it provided the representatives of ethnic minorities with the privilege to occupy the administrative positions within the framework of the autonomous regions. In 1926 a national Swedish village council was created in Gammalsvenskby, the only one in the USSR. In this way, the Swedish colony was for the first time in its history separated administratively from the neighboring German settlements and the separate ethnic status of the Swedes was explicitly recognized. This enabled the Swedes to occupy all administrative positions and, what is even more important, to take decisions at the local level and function as spokesman for the decisions taken locally. All letters from 1928 to 1929 from the inhabitants of Gammalsvenskby to the Soviet authorities concerning the emigration to Sweden were written as official requests of the local organ of power to the regional and central authorities. It was these local authorities that issued the special permission which enabled the pastor Kristoffer Hoas and the farmer Johan Buskas to go to Sweden and to act as their representatives and prepare for the villagers' move there.[62]

---

[61] Andreas Annas, *Livet i Gammalsvenskby*. Unpublished manuscript, accessed August 2, 2010, http: www.svenskbyborna.com
[62] RA. Utrikesdepartementet 1920 års dossiersystem. P 1534, f. 17, Kristoffer Hoas, "Gammal-Svenskby." Unpublished manuscript, 1938, 54 p.

On their return to the USSR, the status of the Swedish national council was reorganized in breach of the norms of the law. The Gammalsvenskby Swedes had to share power with Swedish communists who had come to the village to speed up the construction of socialism there.

In this way, ethnic Swedes again occupied the leading positions in Gammalsvenskby. The Swedish communist Edvin Blom became secretary of the party unit and chairman of the village council. Johan Utas was elected chairman of the *kolkhoz*; shortly to be replaced by the communist Petter J. Knutas. The secret agent of the GPU Alexander Knutas became secretary of the village council. The communist Karl Andersson received the important position of the agronomist of the machine and tractor station (MTS) of Berislav, which served the *kolkhoz*. Hugo Albert Lauenstein was appointed head of the village library and reading room.

A number of other striking differences can be detected in the distribution of power in the Swedish village before the emigration and after it. Before 1929, there were no members of the Communist Party and Komsomol in the village. The inspection carried out in August 1928 by TsKNM noted that "there is no interest in the building of socialism among the villagers; the children are under strong religious influence."[63] The inspection also noted that the inhabitants were highly influenced by the pastor Kristoffer Hoas and his wife Emma even after they had left the USSR for Sweden. Emma Hoas, who was a Swedish citizen, had lived in the village since 1899. Kristoffer Hoas, who was born in the village, had graduated from the Russian-German seminary in Sarata and had worked as a teacher at the Swedish school until 1922. During his stay in Sweden in 1922, he was ordained in Uppsala with a mission to serve in Gammalsvenskby and Southern Russia. His ordination became the cause of a very deep conflict between Hoas (who had no formal theological training) and the German pastor of the Alt-Schwedendorf parish Woldemar Schlupp who had the theological qualifications usually required.[64] In order to prevent the conflict from getting out of hand the authorities gave permission for the registration of a separate Swedish parish. The reason they stated for this decision was that the Swedish villagers said they did not understand German, a claim which was not true.[65]

---

[63] DAKhO, f. R-2, op. 1, spr. 558, arkk.85-94; f. R-2, op. 4, spr. 105, ark. 21.
[64] Wilhelm Kahle, *Geschichte der lutherischen evangelischen Gemeinden in der Sovetunion, 1917-1938* (Leiden: E.J. Brill, 1974), 247–251.
[65] DAKhO, f. R-2, op. 1, spr. 1377, ark. 10.

It was not merely the religious influence of the pastor on his parishioners that mattered. Kristoffer Hoas was the official representative of the Red Cross of Sweden in Soviet Ukraine. All food and economic assistance from Sweden to Gammalsvenskby was distributed through him.[66] Only throughout the period of 1926–1928 Gammalsvenskby received from Sweden the considerable amount of the economic aid in 14,602 rubles in total.[67] The Swedish Red Cross also supported the village dispensary. As a commissioner of the Swedish Red Cross, the pastor negotiated with all Swedish bureaucrats who came to the village as well as with the local authorities. The attempt to limit the pastor's authority was not successful and after a diplomatic intervention, the local authorities had to give all his real estate back to him. This farming economy meant that rich peasants, mill owners and the owners of the largest plots of land wielded considerable influence over the poor.

After a group of the former colonists had returned to the USSR the situation changed drastically. The pastor did not return, the church was closed and turned into a club. The majority of the colonists preferred to stay in Sweden but, under the influence of Swedish communists, several of them joined the party. Woldemar Utas, Petter J. Knutas, Petter E. Utas and Irja Buskas were among them.

An important task of the Soviet policy at this point was the preparation of the young shift of the Communist contractors. In the short term, a *Komsomol* unit was created in the village.[68] The new *Komsomol* members were offered high-ranking positions in the local hierarchy. Lydia Utas became head of the dairy farm. Sigfrid Utas was appointed teacher at the Swedish school. The sport interest group also worked under his guidance. Sigfrid Utas became the first cycle champion of Ukraine.[69] The tractor driver, Johannes Knutas, was given the position of team-leader; he also became head of the local section of the Soviet paramilitary youth organization. In this way in a very short period, the authorities altered the social hierarchy of the Swedish community, and active participants in the communist movement found themselves in the most favorable positions.

---

[66] Hoas, "Gammal-Svenskby," 12–48.
[67] Hedman, Åhlander, *Historien om Gammalsvenskby,* 159.
[68] Viktor Prylutskii, "Molod u suspilno-politychnomu zhytti USRR 1928–1933," *Ukrainskii istorychnyi zhurnal,* no. 4 (2002): 60–79.
[69] Anatolii Andreev, "Khersonets – pervyi chempion po velosportu," *Gryvna-SV,* February 17, 2006, 15.

In accordance with the Bolshevik program of *smychka*[70] the Soviet government, through their consul in Stockholm Vladimir Smirnov, suggested the Swedish communists to draw up a "list of fifteen Swedish comrades wishing to enter the USSR to build the first Swedish kolkhoz there."[71] There is no information whether the list was ever made. But a group of Swedish communists eventually came to Gammalsvenskby. This group included Comintern employees who came to Gammalsvenskby for different kinds of inspections, and students of the Comintern schools sent to the Swedish *kolkhoz* to undergo their summer training. Some of them were sent directly by the SKP. There were also some impostors, Swedish communists who came to the village on their own from other regions of the USSR, after having read about the kolkhoz in newspapers. Most of them came to the village with their families or married in the village. In the archives, the following Swedish communists are mentioned as working in the village: Edvin Blom, Karl Andersson, Hugo Albert Lauenstein, Karl Ture Grääs, Kasper Gustafsson, Hildur Gustafsson, Karl Sigfrid Holmström, Gunnar Blomberg, Erik Karlsson (party alias Karl Johansson), Paul Söderman (party alias Karl Nils Lindroos) and Erik Petersson. Two well-known SKP members, William Heikkinen (party alias Edward Wallin) and Björn Hallström (party alias Red Björn), also planned to settle in Gammalsvenskby, but they did not reach the village.

The biographies of the communists who worked in Gammalsvenskby show that the Comintern and the SKP carefully selected the best-suited candidates. Erik Karlsson and Paul Söderman originated from peasant families, a rare case for members of the SKP. The Swedes who came to the village from Karelia had worked at a greenhouse centre near Petrozavodsk, thus having at least a minimum experience of agricultural work.[72] Karl Andersson was an experienced agronomist, who had worked in Denmark for long periods. The communist Hugo Albert Lauenstein was a blacksmith, whose skills would be in high demand in any *kolkhoz*.

---

[70]*Smychka* means linkage between city and village.
[71] DAKhO, f. R-4033, op. 9, spr. 85, ark. 100.
[72] Gustafson, *Svenska sovjetemigranter,* 47–50.

Document 7: Recommendation of the Politburo of the Swedish Communist Party to comrade Hugo Lauenstein issued by SKP, certified by Edvin Blom. October 7, 1932.

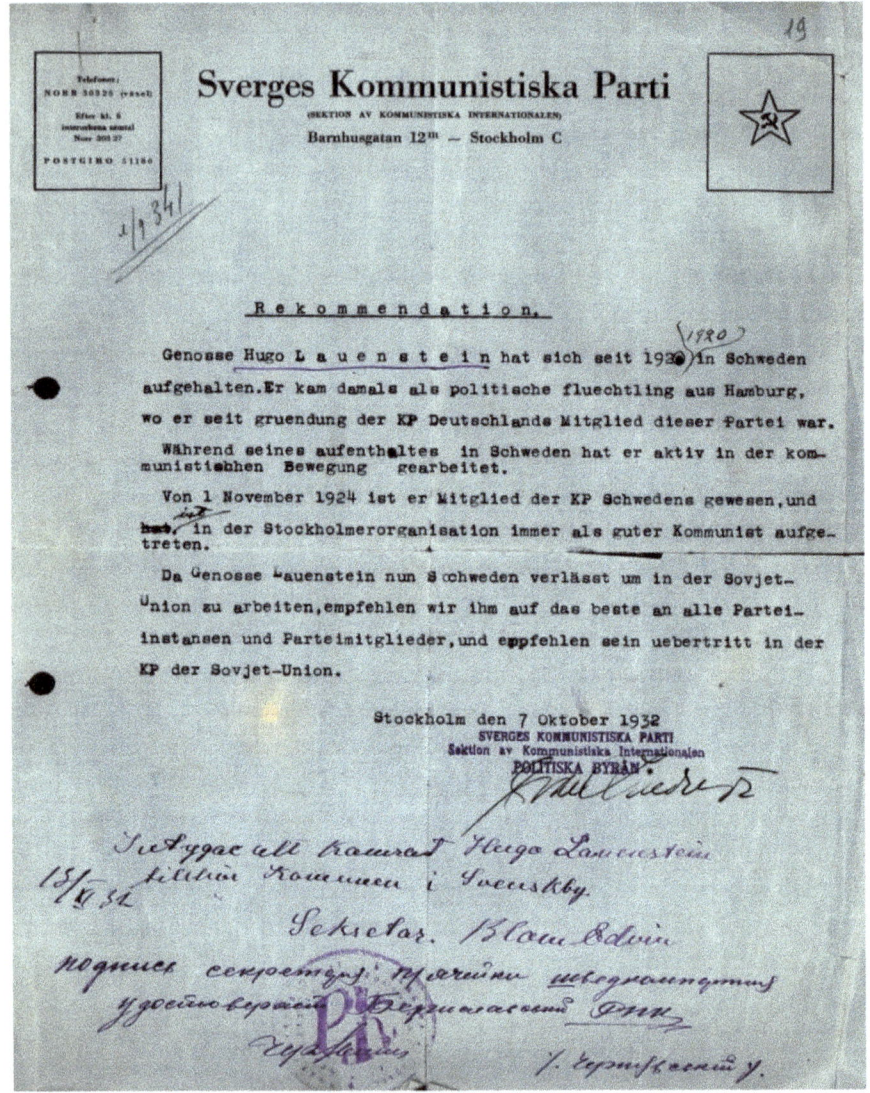

Source: RGASPI, f. 495, op. 275, d. 341.

The Stockholm party organization sent the chairman of the Arbetarnas Svenskbykommitté Kasper Gustafsson to lead the socialist construction in Röd Svenskby. He had been working with the Ukrainian Swedes since they first arrived in Sweden. His wife Hildur Gustafsson, who was also a party member, was supposed to lead the women's movement in the village.[73] However, by the time Gustafssons arrived in Gammalsvenskby, Swedish communists from Karelia, Edvin Blom, Ture Grääs and Sigfrid Holmström, had already taken all the senior positions. They had learnt from the Soviet press about the socialist project in Gammalsvenskby and had come to the village with their families independently of each other. All of them had emigrated from Sweden to Karelia where the construction of the Soviet Nordic republic was underway under the guidance of the Finnish communist Edward Gylling.[74] As a result of the conflict between Kasper Gustafsson and Edvin Blom, Gustafsson and his wife left Gammalsvenskby for Leningrad within a matter of months.[75]

The Holodomor and the strategy of collective resistance

Under the totalitarian system that had been created, the authorities anticipated that the collective identity of the peasants would change quickly and radically. In the work "K voprosam agrarnoi politiki v SSSR" (On the issues of the agrarian policy in the USSR) from 1930 Stalin emphasized that the "collectivization will create a new type of peasant whose psychology has been ploughed up by the tractor."[76] However, the resistance of the Swedish community stalled this process, while the fate of the Comintern project – the Swedish *kolkhoz* – was virtually sealed by *Holodomor*, the great famine that is estimated to have taken 3.5 million lives in Ukraine in the years 1932–1933. The mass arrests that followed crushed all remaining ambitions.

Initially it seemed as if the Swedish colonists were ideally suited for the construction of a prosperous *kolkhoz*. Those who had first gone to Sweden and then returned to the USSR had no land of their own, cattle or real estate. Thus there was no material ground for resistance to the collectivization process. There were no *kulaks* among the Swedes and consequently there was no need for dispossession and deportation. The state helped the Swedish community and gave them a credit of 85 thousand rubles to buy houses and repair them, and to buy cattle. Thanks to the

---

[73] "Till Röda Svenskby för att delta i socialismens byggande," *Arbetar-Kvinnornas Tidning*, 1931:5–6, 8.
[74] See: Nick Baron, *Soviet Karelia: politics, planning and terror in Stalin's Russia, 1920–1939* (London: Routledge, 2007).
[75] DAKhO, f. R-4033, op. 9, spr. 85, ark. 81.
[76] Iosif Stalin, *K voprosam agrarnoi politiki v SSSR* (Moskva: Gosudarstvennoe izdatelstvo, 1930), 8.

Comintern, the *kolkhoz* received a team of specialists, and tractors and trucks from the Berislav machinery and tractor station were made available to the *kolkhoz*. Several young Swedes were apprenticed free of charge as tractor and harvester drivers. The excellent black earth of the Kherson Oblast and the availability of water for irrigation from Dnipro River ensured high productivity in agriculture. The Swedish communist press painted an optimistic picture of the future of Röd Svenskby. For example, in a report from April 1931 there were the following enthusiastic lines:

> The wide and long street runs between the white and beautiful mansions. In the center of the village is the former church, Hoas dopey temple, but on its tower is now the red flag, a symbol of new times above Nya Svenskby [New Swedish village]. The Swedish kolkhoz has got the name of Sveriges Kommunistiska Parti. The kolkhoz owns 765 acres of land. The state has granted a loan of 100 rubles for the purchase of livestock and agricultural machinery. The district government has provided an agronomist and tractors, as well as seeds for the next harvest. The former church is today the people's house, which is equipped with a stage, theatre props and the most modern cinema. In the village there is a reading-room with a Swedish library, a Swedish school, shop, medical center, department of the "Red Help" and "Osoviakhim." The next step will be a huge program of planting vineyards and orchards and the electrification of the village. "Never again Sweden" – say those who have returned and are now awaiting the return of the remaining 200 people still held by the government of Ekman [Carl Gustaf Ekman].[77]

Barely two years later, another Swedish communist who worked in Röd Svenskby expressed a more pessimistic view:

> The machines and the tractors crack one after another, there are no spare parts, and fuel is scarce. The soil has been exhausted. The plan of the state for the procurement of grain is not practicable. Instead of horses, hungry cows are used; as a result, the kolkhoz obtains a quantity of milk in the range of 12–13 liters per day from twenty cows. The food is beyond criticism. The people live on the verge of famine and work only under the most rigid control.[78]

---

[77] "Svensk sovjetarbetare berättar om Röda Svenskby just nu," *Ny Dag,* April 4, 1931, 1, 8
[78] "Svenskarna leva på svältgränsen i Gammalsvenskby," *Borås tidning,* August 4, 1933.

In the absence of a pastor of their own in Gammalsvenskby the Swedes began to visit a German Lutheran church in the neighboring village of Schlangendorf. This is interesting in view of the fact that since the middle of the nineteenth century there existed a painful conflict between the Swedish and German parishioners about the question whether the parish should be divided or not. Following the arrest in 1933 of the last German pastor Friedrich Lang, the role of preacher was assumed by a Swedish woman, Alvina Hinas. In 1935, she was arrested for religious propaganda. In 1937 she was arrested again and executed.

Notwithstanding the fact that the young people appreciated the cinema, many members of the old generation were reluctant to enter the new club, as they believed in "the ghosts who had settled there."[79] The new Swedish school also had some problems. In order to fight religion the school in Gammalsvenskby, like other schools, was open on Sundays and on Lutheran holidays. However, parents tried to keep their children at home on those days, using any pretext. None of the three teachers of the former elementary school of Gammalsvenskby returned from Sweden. It was not possible to train teachers specifically for the school in Gammalsvenskby, the only Swedish school in the USSR. No Soviet textbooks in Swedish were available. The Swedish communists Edvin Blom and Kasper Gustafsson as well their eldest daughters Siri Blom and Wilma Gustafsson worked as teachers without any pedagogical education. Later on they were joined by Sigfrid Utas and Maria Utas (Terenina) who graduated from the class for seven-year olds. While visiting Moscow in the beginning of 1932 Blom offered a position as a teacher to one of the best educated members of the SKP, Björn Hallström.[80] After becoming unemployed in 1934 in Sweden, Hallström sent a letter to the Comintern with a request to be appointed a teacher at the Swedish school in Gammalsvenskby. But the older party comrades talked him out of this idea referring to the famine in Ukraine not covered by the newspapers. Gustav Johansson told Hallström that "the picture he would witness could make a counter-revolutionary out of him, as he would question the correctness of Soviet policy and of Communism."[81]

Thus, having neither qualified teachers nor the necessary literature, the Swedish school could not function normally. When the school was inspected for the first time, its work was found to be unsatisfactory. It used prerevolution literature and Swedish books with portraits of the Swedish Royal

---

[79] Interview with Astrid Lauenstein Bragnum (born 1936), Stockholm. May 10, 2008.
[80] RGASPI, f. 495, op. 275, d. 284.
[81] Björn Hallström, *Jag trodde på Stalin* (Stockholm: Harrier, 1952), 72–73.

family. The pupils could only speak Swedish, and understood neither Ukrainian nor Russian:

> When I [the inspector] asked one student: "Why ... do you not read a Soviet newspaper instead," the answer translated by his teacher was: "We are tired of reading about socialist competition and polytechnic schools."[82]

During the famine in Ukraine in the winter of 1932–1933 the peasants in the Swedish colony were confronted with a dilemma: should they seek assistance from the Soviet authorities or in Sweden? As many other farms in the Kherson district the Swedish *kolkhoz* did not fulfill the exaggerated target for the state grain quota of 1932. As a result the *kolkhoz* Sveriges Kommunistiska Parti was put on a "black list." The whole stock of grain from the *kolkhoz* and the households belonging to it, including the seed for sowing in 1933, was confiscated. The deliveries of foodstuffs to the local shop were stopped. The *kolkhoz* members no longer received any products in exchange for "workday units." The specialists servicing the *kolkhoz* were not paid their wages.[83] In the fall of 1932, the famine came to the village. People survived on potatoes, fish from the river and gophers from the steppe. Virtually all valuable goods from Sweden were sold: bicycles, sewing machines, and clothes.[84]

The members of the party unit approached the regional committee of the party in Berislav with a request for emergency assistance to the village. The request was refused. That meant that the Swedish communists were not able to help Gammalsvenskby. In a conversation with a member of the Berislav district party committee, one comrade Kabakova, Hugo Lauenstein said that "he did not like the Soviet regime; the authorities arrested people – was that communism and freedom; people were dying in their dozens of hunger – was that democracy?"[85]

Conflicts broke out among the Swedish communists. Kristina Sigalet witnessed a quarrel between Hugo Lauenstein and Edvin Blom. Lauenstein cursed Blom and said that "the worms will eat him alive for luring them to such a terrible place."[86]

---

[82]DAKhO, f. 306, op.1, spr. 279.
[83]DAKhO, f. R-4033, op. 9, spr. 85.
[84]Interview with Matilda Norberg (born 1919).Roma, Gotland. August 1, 2008.
[85]RGASPI, f. 495 op. 275, d. 341.
[86] Hedman, Åhlander, *Historien*, 262.

In this critical situation the Swedish villagers resorted to a method used by free Swedish farmers for centuries when living conditions had become too hard or in conflicts the local authorities: a collective legal address to the authorities of the state. This method had been used many times before, by the inhabitants of Dagö in the Swedish empire as well as by those of Gammalsvenskby in the Russian empire and the Soviet Union. There are approximately fifteen earlier examples of such collective letters to the authorities, the first of which was written in the seventeenth century.[87]

In January 1933, the *kolkhoz* members secretly started discussing the possibility of moving to Sweden again. They also considered other possibilities. One idea was to ask for help from the German Consulate in Odessa. Some Swedes did not believe it would be possible to move to Sweden again legally and instead suggested it would be better to cross the Soviet-Romanian border illegally. At one meeting, Julius Hansas declared that "I will not die in this kolkhoz as I hope to get to Sweden through Bessarabia."[88]

Several Swedish women sent letters to relatives in Sweden with stories about the critical condition in the village and begging for help. One example is cited below:

> We have sinned against Sweden and the Swedes and we have shown the greatest ingratitude. But, gripped by debilitating nostalgia for our native home, we did not know what we did,. There is no food in the village, no kerosene. There are only Communist books and other rubbish to buy at the shop. Yes, if you are Christian, you have to forgive us. Please, think of our innocent little children.[89]

In addition, the Swedish communists in Gammalsvenskby sent critical letters to Sweden. On behalf of the SKP Gunnar Granlund informed the ECCI on 19 March 1933 that Hugo Lauenstein in letters to his mother-in-law "writes openly counter-revolutionary things directed against the Soviet Union and especially against Svenskby."[90]

---

[87] Jakob Koit, "De svenska dagöböndernas kamp för sin fri- och rättigheter 1662–1685," *Svio-Estonica* 1951:10, 50–153; Andrej Kotljarchuk, "Nemtsy Ukrainy v sudbakh shvedskoi kolonii na Dnepre, 1805–2007," in *Voprosy germanskoi istorii*, ed. Svetlana Bobyleva (Dnipropetrovsk: Porogi, 2007), 27–35.
[88] DAKhO, f. R-4033, op. 4, spr. 359, ark.131
[89] "Nya nödrop från fränderna i Svenskby," *Norrköpings Tidningar*, March 3, 1933, 7.
[90] RGASPI, f. 495 op. 275, d. 341.

As a result, a virtual bomb exploded in the mass media. On 2 March 1933 the oldest liberal newspaper of Sweden *Aftonbladet* published an article, "Djurkadaver och potatisskal mat i Gammalsvenskby" (Animal carcasses and potato peelings – food in Gammalsvenskby), which reported about the terrible famine and the extremely difficult situation of the Gammalsvenskby inhabitants and Swedish communists. On 3 March 1933 the conservative daily *Norrköpings Tidningar* published an article "Nya nödrop från fränderna i Svenskby" (New cries for help from our compatriots in Svenskby) harshly criticizing the Communist project. The article also discussed concrete measures to help the villagers, for example, individual currency transfers through Torgsin.[91] The Swedish Embassy in Moscow approached the German Embassy in Moscow requesting the Germans to investigate what the real situation was in the village through their consulate in Odessa. The embassy also planned to commission a Norwegian entrepreneur to travel to Ukraine to clarify the situation.[92] The Soviet government was aware of the publications in the Swedish press, probably through their embassy in Stockholm.

The threat of a serious international scandal became real for the Kremlin. It should be noted that the USSR denied the existence of the Ukrainian famine, and there was no information about it in the Soviet newspapers. The Soviet propaganda accused *kulaks* of feigning famine. On 13 March 1933, the political bureau of the Communist Party of Ukraine discussed the situation in the Swedish colony. The Odessa party committee was instructed to take urgent steps to put an end to the famine in Gammalsvenskby. The chief of the Ukrainian GPU Vsevolod Balitsky was ordered "to take measures to introduce immediate measures to stop the information leaks abroad about cases of famine in Gammalsvenskby."[93] The GPU was always quicker to strike; the first arrests in the Swedish colony had already been made on 8 March.

In the beginning of March a list of Swedish villagers who wanted to leave for Sweden was drawn up in Swedish in two copies and sent from the post offices of the cities of Kakhovka and Kherson. The letter from Kakhovka was intercepted by the GPU. The letter sent from Kherson reached the addressee

---

[91] *Torgsin* (Russian: Торгсин) were state-run hard-currency stores that operated in the USSR between 1931 and 1936. Their name was an acronym of "torgovlia s inostrantsami," which means "trade with foreigners."
[92] RA, Utrikesdepartementet 1920 års dossiersystem. P 1534, Del. 3. Diverse biträde åt utlänningar Gammal-Svenskby bor, 1930-mars 1956.
[93] TsDAGO, f. 1, op. 16, spr. 9, ark. 189.

and is today kept in the National Archives of Sweden.[94] The Soviet secret police were totally surprised that the list was signed by virtually all the villagers, including the local members of the Communist Party and *Komsomol*, as well as some communists from Sweden. When the GPU interrogator asked Petter J. Knutas why he, a communist, had signed the list, Knutas replied: "I signed because there are no supplies in the shop and lately I have been eating potatoes without peeling them, and I don't have any bread anymore."[95] Mattias Norberg argued "there is no need for kolkhozes, we keep working but we do not have bread, we are hungry, it is better to run an individual farm."[96] During the interrogation, Alvina Hinas said: "Yes I signed, because we have no bread to feed children, who all the time cry and ask for food."[97] The explanation for the existence of such "anti-Soviet attitudes" among the locals was, according to the investigators, explained by their kulak origin. However, that argument could hardly be used about the Swedish communists. The 47-year-old Hugo Lauenstein, who was a worker and a communist since 1919, a veteran of the German revolution, and furthermore a Swedish citizen said to the GPU investigators: "I signed the list because it was necessary. My personal opinion is that emigration is not a criminal activity, particularly when the villagers are starving."[98] Karl Andersson, who prepared the list, declared "as for me personally, I had no plans to go to Sweden, but my situation is too bad here, I haven't received any wages for three months and that is why I have to leave."[99]

In May 1933, two Ukrainian members of the Polish parliament, Milena Rudnitska and Zenon Pelensky, sent a letter to the president of the League of Nations, the Norwegian politician Johan Ludwig Mowinckel. They wrote that Soviet Ukraine had fallen victim to a catastrophe, a famine unequalled in history. However, the Soviet Union denied the famine and the League of Nations did not take any action. Western-Ukrainian politicians have emphasized that among the victims of famine were representatives of several different European peoples: Swedes, Latvians, Estonians and Poles.[100]

---

[94] RA, Utrikesdepartementet 1920 års dossiersystem. P 1534, Del.3. Diverse biträde åt utlänningar Gammal-Svenskby bor, 1930-mars 1956.
[95] DAKhO, f. R-4033, op. 9, spr. 85, arkk.40–41.
[96] DAKhO, f. R-4033, op. 9, spr. 85, arkk. 36–37.
[97] DAKhO, f. R-4033, op. 9, spr. 85, ark. 38.
[98] DAKhO, f. R-4033, op. 9, spr. 85, arkk. 78–79.
[99] DAKhO, f. R-4033, op. 9, spr. 85, arkk. 21–22.
[100] Vasyl Marochko, "Dyplomatiia zamovchuvannia: stavlennia zakhidnoevropeiskykh derzhav do Holodomoru 1932–1933 v Ukraini," in *Holod-Henotsyd 1933 roku v Ukraini* (Kyiv: Institut istorii NAN Ukrainy, 2000), 154–158.

Despite the measures taken by the GPU, the information about arrests in Gammalsvenskby reached Sweden. The magazine *Vecko-Journalen* published an article by Alma Braathen "Tjekans hand över Gammalsvenskby" (The Cheka's hold over Gammalsvenskby) with a detailed story of the arrests in the Swedish village.[101] Freelance Alma Braathen had visited Gammalsvenskby during her trip to the USSR in July 1932. Sometime later, a number of her reports were published in Sweden. The tone of her articles was quite neutral, but in private talks with some of the villagers she promised to help them to return to Sweden.

Illustration 4: The Truth about Gammalsvenskby.

Source: Magazine Cover. Vecko-Journalen (1932:45). To the article "Sanningen om Gammalsvenskby" (The truth about Gammalsvenskby) by Alma Braathen.

Note: Reporting from a Communist utopia. Leftmost Edvin Bloom, in the center Karl Ture Grääs, rightmost Alma Braathen.

---

[101] Alma Braathen, "Tjekans hand över Gammalsvenskby," *Vecko-Journalen*, no.19 (1933): 20–21.

On 3 July 1933, *Dagens Nyheter* reported about the fate of one of the arrested Swedish communists, Karl Andersson. On 3 August 1933, the largest daily newspaper in Sweden *Nya Dagligt Allehanda* published a detailed critical report about the trial initiated by the GPU against the Old Swedes under the heading: "Gammal-svenskbybor har deporterats av Sovjet! Tjekans process mot svenskättlingarna ny Vickers-affär" (Inhabitants of Gammalsvenskby have been deported by the Soviets! Cheka process against Swedish descendants is the new Vickers trial).[102] On 4 August 1933 *Borås Tidning* printed an article "Svenskarna leva på svältgränsen i Gammalsvenskby" (Swedes live on the brink of starvation in Gammalsvenskby).

On 26 April 1933, a member of the Swedish Parliament and farmer, Gustaf Olsson, wrote a letter to the Foreign Minister Rickard Sandler requesting he intervene on behalf of the arrested Swedish citizens Karl Andersson and Petter E. Utas. According to Gustaf Olsson, he had received a letter sent from Kristina Utas in Gammalsvenskby with an account of the arrests in the village.[103]

The diplomatic intervention by Sweden changed the course of events. The secret police had been planning a big show trial, and the police of the Kherson district arrested seven men and more than twenty villagers were summoned for interrogation. The prosecutor demanded twelve years' imprisonment for the arrested men and confiscation of their property. However, only four of them were convicted by the special GPU court and the sentence they received was three years' exile. The communist Karl Andersson was released and left for Sweden. With the assistance of the Swedish Ministry for Foreign Affairs his wife Maria Andersson (née Utas), who was a Soviet citizen, was given Swedish citizenship and moved to Sweden. However, Petter E. Utas' fate was different. On 18 June 1933 Utas, who had been sentenced to three years' imprisonment, sent a letter appealing for help to the Swedish government. In spite of the support he received from the influential politician Gustaf Olsson, he was denied the right to go back to Sweden. A Swedish citizen since 1931, Utas visited Gammalsvenskby in 1932 as an interpreter and translator for the group of Swedish communists. He was arrested by the GPU, then released but without his Swedish passport. The explanation given was that he had never ceased to be a Soviet citizen and was, therefore, not allowed to renounce his

---

[102] In March 1933, six British engineers, employed by the company "Metropolitan-Vickers," were arrested by the GPU on a charge of wrecking and espionage.
[103] RA, Utrikesdepartementet 1920 års dossiersystem. P 1534, Del.3. Diverse biträde åt utlänningar Gammal-Svenskby boar, 1930-mars 1956.

Soviet citizenship. In 1937, Petter E. Utas was arrested again and disappeared. In fact he was executed following an out-of-court decision by a so-called troika.[104] The Prosecutor General of Ukraine rehabilitated him only in 1999.[105] The place of his burial is still unknown.

The conflict of interests between various Soviet institutions unintentionally benefited the Ukrainian Swedes. When the Holodomor was raging, the GPU tried to limit the contacts the villagers had with foreign countries. However, *Torgsin* employees tried to undo their plans and used to visit Swedish, German and Czech regions urging the people there to write to consulates and relatives abroad pleading for help.[106] The Old Swedes could buy food in *Torgsin* shops in Kakhovka and Kherson for money that they received from Sweden, whether in Swedish *krona* or in other foreign currencies. Alvina Hinas wrote to Sweden after receiving a pound sterling from Gothenburg: "It was an angel of God who came this Easter with a gift to us. For a pound sterling, we got 8 rubles 84 kopecks to buy food."[107]

Thanks to the help from Sweden, the people of Gammalsvenskby could survive the famine without a single death, in marked contrast to the neighbouring Ukrainian and Jewish settlements.[108]

Conclusions

It is impossible to know how the international Communist project in Röd Svenskby would have developed if the *Holodomor* had not hit the village. Before that catastrophe, the authorities were able to bring about fundamental changes in the traditional life of the Ukrainian Swedes within an extremely short period of time. The first stage of the forced normalization of the Swedish villagers brought considerable results. However, the resistance of the Swedes altered the process of change. The rigid food policy of the Soviet government that caused the famine was a manifestation of weakness rather

---

[104] *Trojka* means three-man meeting of the local chief for secret police, party secretary and prosecutor.
[105] DAKhO, f.R-4033, op. 4, spr. 359.
[106] Top-secret report of the chief of Ukrainian GPU Vsevolod Balytskii to the Central Committee of the Communist Party (Bolsheviks) of Ukraine, May 22, 1934 in: *Nimtsi v Ukraini 1920-1930 20 st. Zbirnik dokumentiv*, ed. Bohdan Chirko (Kyiv: Intel, 1994), no. 87; see also: Vasyl Marochko, "Torgsin: zolota tsina zhyttia ukrainskykh selian u roky holodu (1932–1933)," *Ukrainskyi istorichnyi zhurnal* 2003:3, 90–103.
[107] Hedman, Åhlander, *Historien*, 264.
[108] *Z istorii holodomoru na Khersonshchyni u 1932–1933 rr. Dobirka dokumentiv* (Kherson: DAKhO, 2003); Vasyl Piddubniak, *Zhnyvo Molokha. Holod 1932-1933 rr. na Khersonshchyni* (Kherson: KhMD, 2006), 80.

than strength. The government invested large sums in the agricultural sector but the harvests of the kolkhozes were modest. This irritated the authorities, especially compared with the high rate of the budget expense for the agricultural sector. The Ukrainian peasants were left to their fate during the famine. They received no support from outside, and mortality among them was very high. The Swedish villagers were in a better position, not only because of the international status of the Swedish *kolkhoz*. Despite the strict order given to the local authorities to take immediate steps to deal with the famine in the village, the Soviet authorities or the Comintern had done nothing. The rescue came again from Sweden, but it was organized by the peasants themselves. They used the same strategy as they had used for centuries and that enabled Old Swedes to survive the man-made famine without any human loss. Nevertheless, those who had been sentenced to three years' imprisonment in 1933 for organizing the move to Sweden were arrested again in 1937–1938 and executed (except for Alexander Knutas who died in prison in 1935).

The *Holodomor* and the mass arrests put an end to the project of the international Communist movement in Gammalsvenskby. In the beginning of 1934 no Swedish communist remained in the village. A Swedish girl Signe Kaskela met the Holmströms in 1933 in Karelia where she worked in a factory with Svea and Göta Holmström:

> They spoke of terrible distress; they lacked bread, although Ukraine was one of Russia's most fertile regions. However, collectivization had fallen on hard times, and despite the severe drought collective farms were still obliged to provide the required quantity of grain to the state... Svea had scurvy and was bleeding from the gums, and had bruises on her legs. Göta was also starving, but not as badly as her sister was.[109]

The local Swedish communists were expelled from the party for their support for re-emigration. Soon the authorities replaced the leading staff of the village with ethnic Ukrainians. Makar Shurduk became secretary of the party unit, Dmytro Krakovskyi was appointed chairman of the village Soviet, Leonid Shevchenko became head of local *Komsomol*.

There are no indications in the records dating from 1934 onwards that the local authorities and the Executive Committee of the Comintern wished to revive the Röd Svenskby community. This is an important indicator as it

---

[109] Signe Kaskela, *Under Stalins diktatur* (Göteborg: Tre böcker, 1990), 26.

supports the thesis about the total change of the course of the Kremlin in early 1930s from World Revolution to isolation. The institutions set up by the communists, i.e. the Swedish school, the Swedish national council and the Swedish kolkhoz existed technically several years on. However, in the course of the national operations of NKVD in 1937–1938, 23 villagers were arrested and executed. All of them were accused of being members of a fictitious Swedish counter-revolutionary nationalistic spy organization. According to the version of the secret police, the leaders of the organization were Edvin Blom and Hugo Lauenstein who from being communists had become agents of the Swedish intelligence service. Not by pure accident, the active members of the socialist construction were also arrested. Among them the former SKP members Petter J. Knutas and Woldemar Utas, as well as the *Komsomol*[110] members, the chairman of the kolkhoz Johannes Utas and brigadier Johannes Knutas.[111]

The mass terror was followed by the liquidation of all the national administrative, economic and cultural institutes of Gammalsvenskby: village council, Swedish kolkhoz, Swedish school, library, Swedish leisure interest group and choir.

The Swedish national council was abolished by decree of the political bureau of the Central Committee of the Communist Party of Ukraine on 16 February 1938. The reason given was that the existence of national districts and village councils was not justified by the ethnic composition of the population.[112] Taking the floor on the XIV congress of the Ukrainian communists in June 1938 the new regional leader, Nikita Khrushchev, paid particular attention to the work of the hostile intelligence services within the national schools of Ukraine. He said that the establishment of the so-called national schools had been forced upon Ukraine by agents of Western intelligence services and Ukrainian nationalists. However, these schools did not serve educational purposes but were instead turned into nests for counter-revolutionary work. It is striking that Khrushchev mentioned the one Swedish school in Ukraine in the same contexts as he discussed 180 Jewish, 93 Moldavian, 74 Bulgarian and 16 Greek schools. Apparently the Soviet leaders realized that the fate of the Swedes who had returned to the USSR of their own free will, thereby, as it was seen by public opinion in Sweden, betraying their historical fatherland, would be of little concern to the Swedish

---

[110] *Komsomol* (Kommunisticheskii soiuz molodezhi) – the Union of Communist Youth.
[111] DAKhO, f. R-4033, op.4, spr.17, 359, 364, 533.
[112] *TsK RKP (b)-VKP (b) i natsionalnyi vopros*, t. 2, ed. Liudmila Gatagova (Moskva: ROSSPEN, 2005) 378–380.

government. There are no documents in the archives of the Swedish Ministry for Foreign Affairs indicating any reaction to the closure of the only Swedish school in the USSR, the dissolution of the Swedish village council or the, for all practical purposes, ethnic cleansing in 1937–1938.

The fates of the Swedish communists after the Gammalsvenskby project varied. The Berislav committee expelled Karl Andersson and Hugo Lauenstein from the party. After a careful official investigation, the personnel department of the ECCI approved the decision. Their party cards are today kept in Moscow. Erik Petersson and Björn Hallström left the party after their return from the USSR. In 1952 Björn Hallström published the book "Jag trodde på Stalin" (I believed in Stalin) condemning the Soviet regime. Sigfrid Holmström took Soviet citizenship and disappeared in the years of the Great Terror. His daughter Göta Holmström (born in 1917) has since the breakup of the Soviet Union been trying to clarify the fate of her father. His case was discussed during question time in the Swedish parliament in 2010.[113]

For the young Comintern students Erik Karlsson and Paul Söderman Gammalsvenskby became the starting point of a long successful career. They enjoyed the full confidence of the Comintern and the Soviet government. In 1933 Söderman became editor-in-chief of the leading communist newspaper *Ny Dag* in Sweden. In 1936, he was the leader of the party's campaign to mobilize support for Republican Spain. In the mid-1930s Paul Söderman carried out a special mission as a courier in Scandinavia for the foreign section of the GPU. His Swedish passport is kept in Moscow.[114] During the Second World War Paul Söderman was one of the organizers of the Communist resistance, which braced itself for a Nazi occupation that failed to materialize.[115]

Erik Karlsson worked as an agitator among Norwegian lumbermen in the Arkhangelsk region. In 1933, he became a docent, rector of the Scandinavian sector of the Comintern Party School and head of the Scandinavian broadcasting section of the Radio of the Comintern.[116] After the Second World War, Karlsson built an excellent political career in Sweden. For several years, he was a party secretary, a deputy member of the

---

[113] Kirunasvenskarna. Motion till Riksdagen.2010/11:FP1186. Gunnar Andrén (FP), accessed October 28, 2010, http://www.riksdagen.se/webbnav/?nid=410&dokid=GY02XFP1186.
[114] RGASPI, f. 495, op. 275, d. 84.
[115] Jonas Sjöstedt, "Tystnande motståndsmän," *Västerbottens-Kuriren*, May 4, 2009.
[116] RGASPI, f. 495, op. 275, d. 9, ch. 1–2.

Swedish Parliament. He was considered the party expert on agriculture, and he was the author of the first books on the history of the Swedish communist movement and agrarian problems.[117] He died in 1970 glorified as "one of the best known party members, a true Leninist and theoretician of communism."[118] Finally, the leader of the Röd Svenskby commune Edvin Blom remained an active party member until his death in 1953, being at the same time, by a twist of fate, the owner of a farm.[119]

After their return to Sweden almost all the communists, as well as their wives and grown-up children upon return to Sweden, remained silent about their life in Ukraine. Karl Andersson was the only one to break the rule, and he was soon expelled from the party. He gave a series of interviews to the Swedish media about the catastrophic situation in Gammalsvenskby and the famine in Ukraine. In October 1933 the magazine *Sovjetnytt* published the article "Agronom Andersson och Röda Svenskby" (Agronomist Andersson and Röda Svenskby). The authors wrote that because of Karl Andersson, the bourgeois press demonized the Soviet Union and the collective farm project in Röda Svenskby. As a result, a split occurred in the section of *Sovjetunionens vänner* in Varberg where Andersson had "personal accomplices," after it had been decided that a committee should be set up to interview the agronomist about the content of the above hostile publications.

The members of the committee published a report, which demonstrated a fundamental misunderstanding of the nature of Stalin's repressive regime and accused Andersson of incompetence:

> Andersson claims that there is a famine in Ukraine. He also says that despite all difficulties in 1933 Ukraine had a record harvest, the best in 42 years. How this his statement is correlated with information about the people starving in Ukraine? In fact, he sold himself to the capitalists. Was it not his job as an expert agronomist to improve soil quality and racial management of the agriculture?[120]

After the massive repression by the regime in these years, it was no longer possible to resist the annulment of all the rights of the Swedish minority. Since 1933 the population of the Swedish colony was in deep shock. The

---

[117] Erik Karlsson, *Jordbruksfrågor i svensk politik* (Stockholm: Arbetarkultur, 1936); Erik Karlsson, *Lantarbetarna: löner, arbetstid, bostäder* (Stockholm: Arbetarkultur, 1936).
[118] ARAB. Biografica. Vol. 159. Erik Karlsson.
[119] Kaa Eneberg, *Förnekelsens barn. Svenskarna som drog österut* (Uddevalla: Hjalmarson & Högberg Bokförlag, 2003), 156.
[120] "Agronom Andersson och Röda Svenskby," *Sovjetnytt*, no. 10 (1933): 8–9.

kolkhoz named after *Sveriges Kommunistiska Parti* formally existed formally until 1941. In 1943, the Nazis evacuated the population of Gammalsvenskby as *Volksdeutsche* to the Third Reich.[121] In 1945, a part of Swedes (around sixty individuals) emigrated from Germany to Sweden. Another group was deported from the Soviet zone in Germany to the Komi-Gulag.[122] Those who returned found their home village completely changed. In connection with the campaign in 1945 to change the names of the former German colonies, Gammalsvenskby received a new Slavonic name, Verbivka, and soon the colony disappeared entirely as it was included in the new large Ukrainian village of Zmiivka (the former German colony of Schlangendorf). The Old-Swedish *kolkhoz* was renamed, in the typical Soviet manner, after the aviator Valerii Chkalov. After twelve years, the dream of building a little Red Sweden in Ukraine had become a blank spot on the map and in the historical memory.

---

[121] David Gaunt, "Swedes of Ukraine as Volksdeutsche. The experience of World War 2," in *Voprosy germanskoi istorii*, ed. Svetlana Bobyleva (Dnipropetrovsk: Porogi, 2007), 239–250.

[122] Andrej Kotljarchuk, "Ukrainasvenskar i Gulagarkipelagen. Tvångsnormaliseringens teknik och kollektivt motstånd," *Historisk Tidskrift*, no. 1 (2011).

About the authors

SVITLANA BOBYLEVA is a history professor at Dnipropetrovsk Oles Honchar National University, Ukraine. She heads the Institute of Ukrainian-German Historical Studies. Bobyleva has published a multitude of articles on the history of Germans and other foreign colonists in the Russian Empire.

JULIA MALITSKA is a PhD student at the Baltic and Eastern European Graduate School at Södertörn University, Sweden. In 2010 she defended a candidate thesis at Dnipropetrovsk Oles Honchar National University concerning the adaptation of the villagers of Gammalsvenskby to the new judicial and environmental surroundings.

PIOTR WAWRZENIUK holds a PhD in history. He is a researcher at the Institute of Contemporary History at Södertörn University and assistant lecturer at Swedish National Defense College. His current research focuses on Polish military security perceptions in the interwar time and Nazi genocide of Roma in Ukraine 1941–1944.

ANDREJ KOTLJARCHUK holds a PhD in history, is a researcher at the Institute of Contemporary History at Södertörn University and an assistant lecturer at Stockholm University. His present research has centred on the persecution of small minorities in the Baltic and Arctic region in the Soviet Union in the 1930s.

www.ingramcontent.com/pod-product-compliance
Lightning Source LLC
Chambersburg PA
CBHW070544090426
42735CB00013B/3071